The author was born in Manchester, England, in 1959. He was educated at Moorside High School, Swinton. He joined Greater Manchester Police Force in 1980 and was promoted to the rank of Sergeant in 1990. He retired as a Detective Sergeant in December 2010.

He married Janine in 1984 and has two sons, Daniel and Benjamin. Following their marriage to Katie and Elizabeth respectively, the author now has four grandchildren—Phoebe, George, Dylan and Edie—all of whom he adores.

He retired to Spain where he currently helps run a Walking Football Team who raise thousands of Euros for charity.

This book is dedicated to Phoebe May, George Alexander, Dylan David and Edie Rose, (in age order), for when Granddad is no longer with them they may get the opportunity to read this novel and understand a little more about him.

Steve Howarth

BBQ, Beer and Bright Ideas

Austin Macauley Publishers

London • Cambridge • New York • Sharjah

A CIP catalogue record for this title is available from the British Library.

ISBN 9781398411128 (Paperback)
ISBN 9781398411135 (Hardback)
ISBN 9781398411142 (ePub e-book)

www.austinmacauley.com

First Published 2021
Austin Macauley Publishers Ltd®
1 Canada Square
Canary Wharf
London
E14 5AA
+44 (0)20 7038 8212
+44 (0)20 3515 0352

The Sponsors

Los Tres Cafe Restaurante; Multi-Brico; Talleres Horadada; Oakwood Properties; Image Plus Hair Salon; Mar Menor Boats; Caballero Estate Agents; Nautical Horadada and Groupo Trivial.

Each and every one of the donors. Those in Spain, fellow pilgrims en route, the generous residents of Pinar de Campoverde or those just visiting, friends, family and special people in the UK. Not all of the donors knew us, but they took us to their hearts.

The Brilliant Committee

Antonio and Beryl Aguado, Kevin Leonard, Shirley McGennity, Carol Steer, Lorraine and Kevin Connor, Kevin and Christine Jackson and last but not least, Dave and Debbie Coupe and my wife, Janine.

Debbie Coupe, for her research and press liaison.

Señor Emilio Butragueño Santos, for his donation of the signed Real Madrid football shirt.

Johnny and Louise Glennon for their support, use of their Portobello Bar and friendship.

Barry Wright, the Costa Blanca News reporter who ensured that our journey and cause were published weekly, spreading it across the whole of Spain.

Design Right Printers, especially Barry and Gemma for the maps, banners and publicity cheques.

My wife and family for their unwavering love and support, especially Janine, who suffered in silence at such a crucial time in her life.

Finally, to Dave, my "Bruv", without whom my wanderlust would have remained unfulfilled and this fabulous journey would have been nothing more than a pipe dream. Top man!

Table of Contents

BBQ, Beer and Bright Ideas

Hello, my little Couch Pilgrims. Are you sitting comfortably? Then I will begin.

In truth, I have known deep inside that my soul yearns for an adventure, not just gallivanting around the world, but one with a purpose. Not just for me but on behalf of others.

As a detective sergeant in Greater Manchester Police, I had applied for two secondments abroad to satisfy this deep-seated need. The first in the late 1990s was to Bosnia, where I would be under the direction of the UNHCR retraining their depleted and beleaguered police service. The second, in my final years, was a response to a Force appeal for officers, who wished to volunteer to go to Rwanda for a two-week period in order to help build a halfway house for orphans. The latter would have seen me completing a half marathon, with sponsorship, in order to raise funds for the centre. Neither application succeeded and I was left to complete my service, enter retirement, and still have this unsatisfied "wanderlust".

It simply would not go away. I searched the internet for options. Looking after baby orangutans in Borneo appealed but the £3,000 plus it would cost me was out of the question. Syrian refugee camps and other war-torn area were definitely not on the radar for obvious reasons. My family would never forgive me should they ever accede to my pondering and something went wrong in any of those areas. I turned to the Voluntary Services Overseas website, but it was a constant source of frustration. Places which are desperate for help are either far too expensive to contemplate or the tenure at any charitable location is severely restricted. I give Haiti as an example of this. It has been ravaged in recent years by natural disasters, everything apart from a plague of frogs (I'm sorry to any Haitian who may end up reading this, I was not tempting fate nor God himself to deliver this).

Should I have wished to offer my services in that devastated part of the world, it was going to cost in excess of £2,000 for my travel and maybe some basic accommodation? This amount excluded food and inoculations, and incredibly it would only be for one restrictive week. I would spend this limited time helping rebuild social centres or homes for the homeless. Bloody hell, I would have barely hammered a few nails in before I was back at the airport having achieved the square route of nothing. (I wanted to write Sweet FA but it just didn't seem right to swear this early in my account).

There must be tens of thousands of people like me on this planet. Surely I can't be the only one. Perhaps I was just looking in the wrong places.

My retirement took me to Spain and a small village in the southern extremities of the Alicante region called Pinar de Campoverde. An old part of the village was built in the 1960s, however we had bought a holiday home on the new estate which abuts the old village during 2000. It had been a long-term plan to move there permanently, which Janine, my wife, and I eventually did in March 2011. It tore our hearts out leaving our two sons, Dan and Ben, but they were settled with their wives to be, Katie and Lizzie, respectively, and furthermore our grandchildren had not yet arrived. Things may have been totally different, should this have been the case.

During 2015, I joined Pilar de la Horadada Walking Football Team, after all, I was getting old and the aches and pains, that naturally come with age, were arriving in parts of my body I had forgotten existed, not to mention the triple bypass I'd had in 1999, which curtailed any real sporting ambitions I may have aspired to. My one sporting love, golf, was also plagued with a perpetual bad knee. One just has to be sensible (a point I soon forgot in the summer of 2017, but we are getting ahead of ourselves)!

A split in that walking football team arrived and I found myself playing for our local bar or "office", as we prefer to call it, Portobellos. The team is sponsored by the landlord, Johnny, and his wife Louise. A guy called Jim Simpson, together with Dave Coupe and me, undertook the roles and responsibilities of running the club. Jim left prior to the 2017/2018 season for a number of reasons, chiefly, his health although he did not share views that both Dave and I held.

Coupey is another ex-cop from Kent and the NCS (National Crime Squad).

He is a great bloke to know. We soon found ourselves on the same wavelength for almost everything, including the continuity of our club's charity work. From the outset, we had decided that we would raise funds for AECC Cancer and also the Amigos de San Jose Obrero Foundation, which is an

Orphanage in the city of Orihuela some 40 minutes' drive away. The cancer charity is global, whilst the orphanage is local and without a great deal of funding from the government. A good portion of its funding comes from charitable donations.

During last season, 2016/2017, we managed to raise 1,000 euros from our social activities, Quiz Night, Race Night, you get the picture. The proceeds were split equally between the two charities. Mother Superior and one of her sisters from the orphanage arrived at our office for one of the presentations. It's fair to say that we have also collected tools for the orphanage workshops, made up Christmas presents in shoeboxes and taken three cars full to the brim of things for the beach so that the kids can have a holiday for a week. You could not get a postage stamp extra in any of the cars. There were inflatables, new flip flops, bats and balls, towels, sun cream, the works.

The Christmas presents were a little more personal. Beryl and Antonio Aguado, who live on the estate, are closely connected to the foundation and help them and us immensely in coordinating things. In November 2017, Beryl appeared with a bag full of names on pieces of paper. You drew one out. Ours was a boy called Alejandro, 8 years of age. That's all we knew. We would never meet him. Every present was to be squeezed into a shoe box. The reason for this is so that all the children have equal sized presents to open on Christmas day. We set about stuffing ours. Each item individually wrapped to hopefully tease out a little more excitement for Alejandro.

Early summer 2017, May or June, I can't recall. BBQ at ours, although Dave believes it was his. Clearly, the alcohol we drank has had some effect or it's just our age. I'll choose the latter. But yes, on this particular occasion, David, I and our company had drank sufficient to loosen our tongues. This seems to come with the territory here in Spain.

Dave had barely got the words, 'I fancy doing the Camino,' out of his mouth, when I immediately said, 'Count me in, I'd love to do that.'

I knew straight away he was referring to the "walk" between San Jean Pied du Port in France to Santiago de Compostela in Northwest Spain. The small but very significant snowball had started its rapid journey down the snowy slopes of our ambitious minds.

We decided to start training in October. There were several reasons for this. The heat of the summer would have dissipated by then, the local roads would be quieter without the tourist traffic and we both thought that six months would be ample. We would not train together either. Simply put, what the heck would we have to talk about for 35 days if we had already exhausted every topic, let alone the countless "Keystone Cop" stories we were too prone to recounting at any given opportunity. No, the sensible thing to do would be to train alone. We both agreed that we would carry an old rucksack. To start with, there would be two litres of water inside, which equates to two kilograms. We would be carrying nine or ten kilos on the Camino. Each month we trained, the litres would be increased by one to let our bodies acclimatise. Yes, I know my maths isn't too clever. Two kilos in October, plus one, plus one, etc, amounts to seven kilos. We would both end up with eight during March.

Now, Campoverde is on a hill. It's a few hundred feet above sea level. I know this for certain, as I can see the coast several kilometres away. Not only can I see, but I've just stopped writing to check how high above sea level it actually is. To be precise, it's 520 feet above. Not a big hill but I thought that would be plenty to train on. How naive was I?

Things started off on the training front, relatively sedately. The first of October just ten kilometres from my home to Rebate and back. This route took me along a winding country road, inland, through the local pine forests. It also contained some modest hills or "bumps in the road", as I've retrospectively Christened them. Two kilos in my rucksack I set off on that first Sunday morning. A spring in my step, fully focused on where all this would lead and a smile on my face. The warm, late summer sun teasing beads of sweat out of every pore and I hadn't walked a kilometre yet!

I hadn't given much thought to my attire in truth. Old Rockport boots I'd had since 1994, which I bought in one of those "outlet malls" whilst on holiday in Florida. Socks, two pairs, shorts, (more for the beach than walking), T-shirt and a fluorescent, yellow, plastic, long sleeved top, just so that motorists could see me. Just hang on a minute, plastic, long-sleeved top! No wonder sweat was pouring out of every pore. Irrespective of this mental awakening, I was to wear this top on every single training walk no matter what the temperature was. I wasn't subject of a "hit and run" and it helped keep a little weight off.

You can drive to Rebate and back in a little over ten minutes. It took me one hour and 58 minutes. I was quite chuffed at this. Marginally over five kilometres per hour for my first walk, hooray! It would hardly deviate from 5 kph for the next six months. I had found my pace early. The walk itself was pleasant. Locals going to Sunday markets or just out for a drive would slow down, horns honked, and sunburnt arms and hands waved from open windows. The word was out. No going back now. I have to confess that there was just a little lead in my legs as I approached the house. I was ready for a rest and good drink of water, even though I had drank a little en route.

Bugger me, wouldn't you know it! I approached my gate only to see it open before I'd had chance to get the key out of my pocket. It was my wife, Janine. Elmo, our Catalan Sheepdog on the lead at her side, 'Fancy a walk into the village?'

Who could resist? My options were a) A quiet afternoon with Jan sulking, after all, I'd had two hours on my own, or b) just another sweaty two kilometres with a small beer at halfway in the village. Ahh, beer! My dry mouth was suddenly flooded with saliva. Although I must admit the thought of thinking I was deaf for part of the afternoon also had some appeal. I was grateful for that first test. It focused my mind and I had enjoyed it. I knew what lay ahead regarding the training, well, sort of.

I would often see Dave on his training walks too. Earphones in, cap with a sun protector for his neck, 'head down, arse up,' as the saying goes.

My training was done in earnest and with a schedule, as was Dave's. At least three walks per week with the shortest being a brief 10k. It was difficult finding different routes to prevent boredom setting in. 20 kilometres to Rebate, the return and then add a trip to the Rio Seco, before returning home. The Rio Seco is a beautiful 3.5k stretch of dry riverbed in a sandstone gorge. It's a popular local walk for dog owners and strollers alike.

17 kilometres to El Mirador and back. A stop at the halfway point at Café Vaguada for Tostados con Tomate or Bocadillo con Lomo y Huevos (tomatoes on toast or pork and egg baguette). This was my "Saturday" route and during my numerous visits to the café, I found myself speaking Spanish to a waitress called Maria. She was always interested in the training regime and often enquired about the starting date of the Camino. I only had to open the door and she would ask which snack was my preference of that day. A point I've discussed with several people since going to this cafe is 'why are Spanish eggs so golden and so tasty?' a theme that would resurrect itself some weeks later. Honestly, eggs sold and eaten in the UK are crap. Pale, tasteless and a complete culinary failure in comparison. Just my opinion.

Another training route was via the Rio Seco, down to the coast at Rio Mar and back. This trip was 24 kilometres, with the last two hours being uphill or up 520-foot bump. On one such walk, I was joined by a friend, Carol Steer, her two friends, Gilly English (what a great name; she should have been a Bond girl!) and Mary Burrell. They were holidaying with Carol. There was also my wife, Janine and our dog, Elmo. The three ladies, not that my wife isn't one, were some years older. The "walk" was more of a guided tour. I pointed out the wildlife as we walked. A variety of birds, lizards, butterflies and flowers. They took photographs and walked the first half to a beach bar. Now, there's a lovely place to take a break. We all had a drink and then they handed over the very first donation for the future Camino walk. October hadn't even come to an end yet. The ladies returned to Campoverde using Carol's car, which we had dropped off in a local side street earlier.

We all know that the sea has a lure and when it's coupled with a beautiful beach and clear blue sky, it's irresistible. The mental fortitude it took Janine, Elmo and myself to drag ourselves away and return "up bump" to Campoverde was immense, but hey, I'm in training! Now Elmo is a sheepdog, four years of age and with boundless energy. We walked the legs off him that day, fleetingly. I say fleetingly, as when we returned home, he drank water, fell asleep for all of 30 minutes and then brought several toys to my feet so that I could throw them for him to fetch. (See pic of Elmo). Seriously! What is in dry dog food?

All of these walks started and finished at home. Some were merged with others to extend the training. But as my house is on top of the hill, no matter where I walked, the last stretch was always the most testing.

There were many things to take my simple mind away to exotic places whilst I trained. As you will read throughout my account, I am an avid birdwatcher, feathered variety. I am not a true "twitcher", where they travel the length and breadth of a country to glimpse a rare bird, which has been blown off migration by exceptional trade winds. No, I merely find them all fascinating. Their plumage, nest building, courtships, feeding and migration habits are all grist to the ever-turning mill in my mind. What's more, it brings out the "detective" in me, should I fail to identify any bird that crosses my path. Books out, and I have quite a few, off I go. Concentration on habitat, size, distinguishing marks etc, etc. All this is due to my granddad Walker. Probably the finest man I ever knew. I say this in the knowledge that this honour would have gone to my dad, however he passed away before I was 12 years old. He was a compositor for the newspapers at Thompson House in Manchester. This meant he worked nights constantly and my time with him, sadly, was restricted to say the least. Don't get me wrong, I love him beyond words, I always will, and he will feature later.

But before I get back to the thread of this account, I have to bring up one topic relating to the death of our dad in 1972. Whilst my sister, Ann, and I have pictures by the hundred and some fond memories, I cannot hear my dad's voice. It's a simple but basic thing that nowadays distracts me when I have time. People ten years younger than me will have videos, DVDs and heaven knows what else in the future with family holidays, full sound effects recorded for time immemorial. You lucky sods. Although I should now count myself as fortunate too because of the invention of Skype and FaceTime, because this gives us permanent contact with our two sons and four grandchildren. However, no matter how I try or what voice my mind concocts, I will never hear my father's voice.

Reverie over and back to Granddad Alex Walker. What an incredible and inspirational man. Quite short, say 5'6", not an ounce to spare, although remarkably statuesque in physique. Grey-white hair swept back and calm, collected and thoughtful in manner. He was special. He never said anything that wasn't relevant, to the point and always correct. His tone barely changed, and his boyish smile was completely beguiling. He had been in the fire brigade, based at Eccles in Manchester and had been instrumental in bringing about the Fireman's Union. He had become a master plasterer, following the fire brigade, which very nearly took him to New Zealand to lecture but the emphysema, caused by the plaster dust, would bring about his demise far too early for me. He was a gentleman of a bygone age and took over my dad's role post the 19th of September 1972, the day when my father passed away from a heart attack aged 36. My triple bypass I mentioned earlier was due to the same condition, familial hypercholesterolaemia (too much fat in your blood, which clogs up your arteries, in layman's terms).

My granddad was the inspiration for my love affair with birds. We would walk for miles. Even from the age of six or seven, we would be out on Barton Moss or anywhere in the open, it didn't matter. Birds identified, trees climbed, nests inspected and materials used noted, eggs counted and the yearly cycle observed in detail every day of my young life. I could write a book about my lovely granddad, but I would have to leave out his politics. As you'd guess, he was a staunch Labour supporter, whilst me, well, I was one of Margaret Thatcher's boys. Politics was not a subject to be discussed with my granddad, although my nana used to throw in the odd proverbial "hand grenade" now and then when being a little mischievous. No, my granddad and I had too much love to share to let this topic blight our relationship and we both knew it. One short story I recall was when I was only seven or eight years of age. Back to Nana and Granddads after school to their flat, just off New Lane in Eccles. Out and about on my own, two storeys below, just minding my own business when an object on the grass at my feet took my attention. I prodded it with my toe. It didn't move or spring to life. I bent down for closer inspection. It was a dead starling, I can still see it now. It's head severed from its body. A bloody cat, God, I dislike cats, must have caught it for its sick sport, not because they are ever hungry. Anyway, I picked up its head and inspected it. Open and closed its beak, noted it's almost black, speckled, iridescent plumage and never thought a thing about it as I deposited it in the pocket of my grey school shorts.

A few minutes later, a shout from my nana and off I went, bounding up the stairs two at a time. I was hungry and ready for tea.

Fed and watered it was time for my bath. Bath times were great at Nana and Granddads. Lots of bubble bath and icebergs of foam made by me sliding up and down to my heart's content. It was all going swimmingly but unbeknown to me, my simple little world was about to shatter around me. It still is the most cataclysmic shriek of doom I've ever heard. I thought the small block of flats had started to crumble beneath my cosy bath. It had come from my lovely nana, although I don't believe I would have found her particularly endearing or lovely at that given moment. She had been emptying my shorts pockets before placing them in the wash. I now know that she only ever expected to find tissues or the odd sweet glued to the fluff and other detritus you'd find in any boy's shorts. She certainly didn't expect to find a severed Starlings head! Apparently, her fingertips hadn't identified it deep in my pocket so, duty bound, she brought it out into the daylight. I believe she nearly fainted but composed herself enough to shout, 'What the bloody hell! Alex! Come here!'

As if HE were to blame! It may be a slight exaggeration, but when my granddad entered the bathroom seconds later to see me, looking up, mouth open and with doleful eyes, he merely said, 'You've nearly killed your nana with that bloody birds head! What bird was it, anyway?'

'Starling,' I replied.

He smiled as only he could, turned his back to leave and sternly said, 'Get dry and ready for bed.'

I swear I could see him grinning. He wasn't stern at all.

And now here I am, identifying foreign birds to three (four) lovely ladies sauntering down a sandy path alongside reed beds eight to ten feet tall. I pride myself at the moment as I've started to learn the Spanish names of these birds, only a few, but it's a start, even at my age. You will read later that I did this for Dave's benefit some months later on the Camino. Well, I think he pretended to be interested.

It's surprising what you find on the roadside whilst training. No dead starlings but other corpses of interest. I passed a red legged partridge in a dry culvert on my way out to Rebate one morning. I mentally noted the exact spot. On the return journey, I crossed the road, bent down and picked up the dead bird. Immediately, I was seven years of age again. There wasn't a mark on it. Rigor Mortis had not set in and there were no insects or flies on it depositing their eggs which would later turn to maggots. Do I or don't I? That was the question. I did. Rucksack off, opened up and partridge deposited amongst the three, litre bottles of water. Once home, showered and moderately hungry, I set about plucking the bird. It only took a few minutes. There wasn't even a bruise on the carcass. It must have been struck in the head, a part I wasn't interested in, and which now no longer attached itself to its body. I gutted it using my butchery skills gained at HG Poole's Butchers on Moorside Road in Swinton. A part time job I'd taken as a 15-year-old in order to buy my school uniform post my father's death.

I cosseted the naked partridge in foil and placed it in a very hot oven. It was lovely. Cooked to a turn and gamy. Now, my wife is not known for eating road kill or indeed enjoying meat from "game" in any form but I have to say, even knowing the source of this culinary delight, she actually ate and savoured the meat. Hallelujah!

Strangely enough, all the deceased animals I've found whilst training were on this same stretch of road. The drivers of Campoverde must have stickers on their cars just like fighter pilots of an earlier age. There was a dead snake, possibly a lesser smooth snake and a large, iridescent blue, lizard. Well, I say lizard but in truth it was mostly its skeleton.

I also found two other objects on the road to Rebate. One was a resin turtle about two inches in length and the other was a set of wooden rosary beads with a crucifix attached.

I picked up the turtle for one reason. Some days before, we happened to be back in Manchester, helping my son Dan and his wife Katie with babysitting duties for my grandson, George. They had just had their second child, a beautiful girl, Edie. Any excuse for me to have a cuddle and see them other than on FaceTime.

Anyway, I found out that George was into "The Blue Planet", and had started naming the sea creatures, particularly his favourites, sharks. One day, post fourth viewing of the aforementioned programme, we got out the Lego, which was contained in a large, green box in the shape of a Lego brick. Blow me down. He took the lid off with its eight raised connecting circles. He lay face down on the lounge carpet, placed the lid on his back, imitated the breaststroke, and said, 'Look, Granddad. I'm a turtle.'

The pride in me nearly exploded out of my chest. Now there's a chip off his granddad's block! The resin turtle I had recovered from the tarmac I made into a key ring, which subsequently adorned my rucksack throughout the Camino. It's still there now. One day, when I've faced the same demise as the starling, partridge, snake or lizard, I would like George to have that keyring and to understand its poignant significance to both him and me.

The rosary beads and crucifix I truthfully tried to ignore. I've never considered myself as a religious person and subsequently left them on the roadside. It must have been fate for the very next time I took to that road; they were still there. I had given their existence some contemplation in the interim and had decided, prior to finding them again, that if they were still there, then I would pick them up. I knew exactly what I was to do with them. I knew, because I was now actively studying the Camino and found that there was a 50-foot crucifix, La Cruz de Ferro, amongst hundreds of thousands of "Pilgrims Stones" on top of a mountain called Monte de Leon. It's a key point in the Camino journey. I simply knew, deep in my heart, that not only was I going to write "For Our Dad" and "Ann (my sister) and Steven" on the back of it, but I was going to tie it to that cross when the moment came, and place it, pride of place, amongst all the other objects which adorn it.

I may not be too religious, but I am emotional.

The training gathered pace and the litres of water increased by the month. The residents of Campoverde all seemed to be involved in "Dave and Steve's Camino". They were not only waving out of their car windows or honking their horns as they passed but they were pulling alongside and asking me how far I had walked and still had left to go. They knew that Dave and I had provisionally decided to commence the Camino in early April and as that month approached, I constantly heard, 'Not long now.'

On one training day, I had not long set off when a white van, driven by a local bloke called Paul, passed on the other side of the road. I saw the window of the van open and his head appeared. 'Get a f*****g life!' he shouted.

I knew he was pulling my short and weary leg and could hear him bellow with laughter as he drove off.

One other key aspect of the Camino were the charities and how we set about fundraising. Dave and I decided that it was too much work for the two of us on top of all the training, so we set about forming a committee. In all, there were 13 of us. I shall name them all now and give them our eternal thanks.

In no particular order, they were Lorraine and Kevin Connor, Christine and Kevin Jackson. These four were also the foundation of the Portobello Walking Football Social Committee. Then there was Kevin Leonard (and no, you didn't have to be called Kevin to be a member of the committee), Carol Steer, Shirley

McGennity, Beryl and Antonio Aguado, Debbie Coupe, my wife Janine, Dave and myself.

We met once per month at my house, where fundraising quiz nights, Mr and Mrs Night, coffee and cake morning, the Great Big Send Off Party and the incredible "Welcome Home Party" were all brainstormed and put into action. Raffle prizes were somehow conjured up with contributions from well meaning friends and neighbours. Gift boxes the size of hampers were made up by Beryl using a variety of goods. They were beautifully wrapped and presented in baskets.

Antonio also played a blinder. Apparently, he is a good friend of Señor Emilio Butragueno Santos, a former Real Madrid striker, who is still working for the club. Promises of a fully signed up Real Madrid shirt were muted, but in truth I was a little sceptical. I clearly had no idea of Antonio's connections. In one of the early meetings, it appeared. Antonio walked up the steps to my house with a beaming smile. He held out his arms. I thought he wanted a hug as a greeting, but there it was hidden in a small gift bag from the Real Madrid supporters' shop. I couldn't believe my eyes as I lifted out the shirt to see the signatures of the entire first team squad, Ronaldo, Ramos, et al. I could see that each player had also included their squad number, alongside their signature, because in truth, they may well have been doctors as their scrawl was completely indecipherable.

Antonio whispered in my ear as the bag exchanged hands, 'I've already had a bid for 1,000 euros,' he said with that typical boyish smile and a glint in his eye.

WOW! What a start to the fundraising. In order to authenticate it, the shirt also came with an email between Antonio and Butragueno.

Just a little Camino information here, "Butragueno" was known as "The Vulture" whilst he played. He has an incredible record, having won almost every major honour with both club and country. I would like to take this opportunity to say a great big "Thank You" to a man I am never likely to meet, for his compassion and generosity. You will read more later in this book about the shirt and it's auction during the "Welcome Home Party". I had to guard that shirt with my life during the following weeks, especially when I took it out with me one Saturday evening. No, even I am not that brazen to wear it for a social event.

The reason I "took it out" was because in our local town there is a Peña, a club, which just happens to be a Real Madrid Supporters Club. Cheekily, I thought that I could bump up the auction value by hawking it around. I took

Ricardo and Pauline with me in order to translate. They were neighbours a few years ago who are now close friends. Ricardo is from Navarra in Northern Spain, whilst Pauline is his English wife. I would walk through the Navarra region a few months later during the Camino.

Anyway, back to Saturday night. We had to ring a bell on the first-floor door before we were given admittance. After a brief explanation of our purpose, we were taken to a bar inside. We ordered cokes and waited for a few minutes before a man arrived and escorted us via a function room, where 50 or so elderly Spaniards were playing "Bingo", and into a back office. A man called Emilio, how appropriate, greeted us. Thankfully, he spoke English very well. I produced the shirt, and whilst his eyes lit up, he shook his head as we spoke. He explained that he was the right person to approach regarding the auction of the shirt but there was no way he could spend in excess of 1,000 euros of the club's money so frivolously. He would however ensure that the wealthier members of the club were made aware of its existence pending the auction on the 31st of May. I left my details, should anyone show any interest.

As things seemed to be progressing nicely, Dave and I decided to finalise dates for leaving Campoverde, travelling to Pamplona and onto San Juan Pied du Port, where we would start the Camino.

The Farewell Bash was to be on Thursday the 5th of April. I will come to that in a while. We would take the train from Murcia on the morning of Friday, the 6th, arriving in Pamplona that evening via a one stop/change at Atocha Station. On Saturday, the 7th, we would travel by coach to San Juan Pied du Port in France, have a day's rest and set off on "our jolly boys outing" on Monday, the 9th of April. Our plans were not written in stone, not yet at any rate, but they gave Dave and me focus. I have referred to the incredibly hard task of walking the Camino as "a jolly boys outing" because of the attitude of one or two so called friends in the village. It is not for me to say whether people should contribute to our charities nor indeed what they should think but I will not have them thinking that this Camino, OUR Camino, was anything but toil, sweat, perseverance, dedication and a bloody hard slog in the aid of two important charities. Not to mention the 2,000 euros each that Dave and I would spend, out of our own pockets, on equipment, travel, accommodation, food and yes, beer and wine. The latter I firmly believe we were entitled to at the end of each and every walking day (beware any "would be pilgrims"! It ain't cheap to walk the Camino and we did not stay in pensions, hostels or hotels every night!).

The committee continued doing a great job whilst Dave and I toiled during our ever increasing mileage in training. Small buckets, ten in all, were purchased from one of the many Chinese shops in the area. I produced a brief synopsis of what Dave and I proposed to do, the fact it was for the two charities and how long the walk would take. I arranged for Beryl to do a translation and printed them both off with photos of Dave and myself. All were laminated and secured to the buckets using Sellotape and Velcro, after all, I am of the early Blue Peter brigade.

They were placed in ten optimal premises, or so we thought, where they could be left for people to make donations of "loose change", referred to in Spain as brown money, one cent, two cent and five cent pieces. The first premise was obviously "our office", Portobellos. There was a new a swanky hairdressers called "Image Plus", Glens Den which was a second hand shop, a bar called The View, the local Iceland store, Gama store, The Rusty Nail pub, Juanita's Pizzeria, Matilda's Estanco shop and Maggie O'Brien's Bar.

Should any of the residents of Campoverde read this account, if it's ever published, let me tell you that each and every one of you who made a donation, are incredible. It soon became obvious that these people had taken Dave, me and our cause, to heart. The buckets were visited and opened every week or so. The contents removed, counted, recorded and banked. Blimey Charlie! Twenty, Ten and Five Euro notes were there, along with every other denomination of coin. There was even Sterling currency from well meaning holiday makers. Just a note regarding this. The Sterling currency subsequently went into the British Armed Forces Poppy Appeal collection box in our "office".

We were off to a fantastic start, although the 10,000 Euro target Dave and I had secretly set seemed a long, long way off. On one amazing week, there was over 160 euros in the bucket at Image Plus Hairdressers. Well done, girls, but Sharona, you're clearly not charging enough for your services! True or not, "Sharona" is THE girl featured in the song "My Sharona" by the Knack, recorded in April 1979 and released in June. You have to be of a certain age to recall this iconic song from the brilliant Punk era. Legend would have it that she was dating a member of the band at the time they wrote the song.

During the few months of training, there were the inevitable breaks for a week or so. The first was a speedy return to the UK regarding a health matter. My "call to arms" came for me during a phone call at 2pm one afternoon. Conversation finished, and in a flap, as I had to return ASAP. We interrogated the options provided on the internet sites. Bingo! Flight into Liverpool Airport on Blue Sky Airlines, sorry, never heard of them, but leaving Alicante, an hour's drive away, at 6:30pm! Booked, packed and at Alicante airport by 4:30pm. When the call comes from your family, absolutely everything is dropped. Arrangements had also been made with my son, Ben, for him to pick me up at Liverpool airport.

I have to say that whilst I had never heard of Blue Skies that they were really good. Punctual, free hot or cold drinks and as many Flapjacks as you could eat, oh yes, and cheap.

Ben was there, as promised. Bottle of water and chocolate waiting for me in the car off we went on the 25-minute journey. Time to catch up with his family's latest adventures en route. I was back in Manchester by 10:30pm. Not a bad turn around!

The only other break in training was due to a cold and chest infection. Even though both breaks were for a week or less, I found it really can be quite difficult to go out straight away and walk 24k. No, better take it easy, just 17k with five litres on my back for the first one back.

At this point of writing, I am trying to ensure that I do not miss anything at all regarding the training or the fundraising. So now, I will turn my attention to the latter.

Thursday night is the quietest night for Johnny and Louise at Portobellos' so like all good customers, we decided our events would be on these evenings to return our support.

First there was the Quiz Night. It was packed. I'd had a map of the Camino printed on a board by the "Design a Right Company" with each of the 32 stages marked thereon. Together with our charity banners, they adorned the walls. What a brilliant night. Quiz, raffle and several games of "Play Your Cards Right" brought in almost 300 euros.

The Mr and Mrs Night a couple of months later was a hoot. Virtually every couple joined in just to show how little they actually knew about each other. Lorraine, the compère, did a great job. Jan couldn't take part, so Shirley McGennity, from the committee and I just did it for a laugh whilst seated at our own table. I'm not just saying this, but we only got one question wrong about each other and we've only really known one another for less than two years. We would have walked it. Maybe that shows at our age and with 34 years of marriage behind us, you forget more than you remember.

This evening too brought in over 300 euros. The "pot" was growing at an unbelievable rate.

And now I must recount the incredible "Coffee and Cake Morning".

During earlier committee meetings, Beryl Aguado had mentioned that she had been previously involved in "Coffee and Cake" mornings for other worthy causes. The chief piece of intelligence she gave us was the fact that they raised 600 euros. It was definitely worth a try and so this became our next fundraising project. Our house is situated across the road from a small but adequate community centre, which sits amongst trees, bushes and a small children's play area. It has a small car park and plenty of paved area on which to set the tables and chairs.

This was to be the venue. The date we set was Saturday, the 24th of March.

We would limit the numbers to 100 people with the tickets that were to be printed going at five euros each. Christine Jackson said that she would run a tombola stall, there would be a bric-a-brac stall, with items being donated for this from friends, team members and residents of Campoverde. The good ladies of the committee and their friends would bake cakes and donate them free of charge and some of our funds would purchase coffee, tea, sugar, milk and cordial, etc.

I made a visit to our local "Town Hall", which is nothing more than an office in our village. I booked the community centre and tables/chairs. It was all going swimmingly!

The highs and lows of bric-a-brac. Let me tell you that people have some very different ideas regarding what is and isn't bric-a-brac! Four, yes four, flat screen televisions of various sizes were donated. Shirley McGennity donated one and even went to the trouble of buying a new remote for it! There was a brand-new Nissan roof rack, sets of golf clubs, brand new, in the box an electric pizza oven, new microwaves, golf club carriers, not forgetting the Capo de Monte floral candle holders. It simply was mind blowing. These items were far too good and valuable to be called bric-a-brac and so we decided to have an auction for them instead during the morning.

However, that was the upside! Other donations included old worn out cushions, dirty broken pots, pans and crockery. Some of the crockery was chipped or cracked. There were cool bags for picnics which had seen better days and subsequently saw the bin. It was as if people, in some instances, simply wanted to rid their homes of the detritus that had built up over the years. We had to be careful as it was likely that these well-meaning residents would also be attending the function. Separating the "wheat from the chaff" would be a delicate operation for the keen-eyed ladies of the Committee. The collection of "stuff" became a storage problem. There was simply too much arriving at our house. People with carloads were turning up daily. We subsequently contacted our neighbour, Liz, and she, very kindly, offered her house as a storage depot.

As we transferred the items, they were placed into areas ie electrical, pottery, soft furnishings, pictures, books (books by the hundred). You get the idea.

The Saturday approached and all of the volunteers knew their responsibilities.

The tickets had sold like hot cakes if you'll pardon the pun and all seemed to be going to plan. You know by experience that something, no matter how small or large, would go wrong. We simply would not get the benefit of feeling a job had been well done if we did not have a crisis or two. This Coffee and Cake morning would be no different.

Several days before the event, the wind picked up, not just a breeze but a 35 to 40 mph of wind. Branches off trees, the tables and chairs from the local bars blown down the road, canopies furled back. I constantly had my beady eye on the Accuweather website. There didn't seem to be much change for the coming Saturday. Maybe fate or divine intervention would grace Campoverde, or at least our small part of it when the time came.

Friday arrived and I noticed that there had been no activity at the community centre. I went to the "Town Hall" to collect the keys. I was given a set by the lady in the office, who told me that should they not be the correct ones, I was to return and she would issue me with another bundle. Thankfully, they were and I entered the centre, which also doubles as a police office. There were a few chairs and a couple of tables but nothing like the numbers I had ordered some weeks before. I returned to the lady in the office and explained the problem. She took out my order form from a file, checked everything was written down correctly and made a phone call to the main Town Hall in Pilar de la Horadada. Now, please bear in mind that it is now 1pm on a Friday and there's a siesta at 2pm and very little work thereafter as the Spanish prepare for weekend.

The phone call seemed to take an age and considerable panic was building in the pit of my stomach. Surely, they wouldn't bugger up all our hard work? One 45 post meridian and I'm back at the community centre, pacing up and down like an expectant father again. One truck, three men in Council overalls and the correct number of tables and chairs duly arrived at 1:55pm. They were cutting their siesta fine. I could breathe again, well, almost; the wind was still a major concern.

I didn't sleep much that Friday night. The sound of the constant wind and it's seemingly hourly increase in strength had my mind in a whir. Setting up at the centre was out of the question, everything would simply be blown away. What to do? Every detail of the military planned operation was unravelling minute by minute. Would we have to cancel it? Surely, people would understand? What about all the cakes that had been baked, all the effort people had gone too? No, absolutely not. Time for plan "B". The helpers were meeting me at 8am at the Centre in order to set it up. We had just enough time. Kevin Leonard, Kevin Connor, Danny Lennihan, Coupey and I sprang into action. The 100 chairs and 12 large tables were hauled by hand the 50 or so yards into our back garden. With the inclusion of our own patio furniture, we would have enough tables and chairs to set up the bric-a-brac stalls under our car port, the

Tombola inside the front gate and the rest around the pool in the rear garden where people could sit, enjoy their coffee and cakes and chat with their friends. The rear of our house is isolated from most winds by ten-foot-high walls. And whilst the wind was still howling outside, it was barely a breeze in the gardens of our property.

Everyone concerned, to coin a phrase, "pulled their tripe out" on that morning. A notice was quickly scrawled and sellotaped to the front gates of the community centre. Coupey, in a moment of inspiration, stood in the road and redirected cars to the front of our house. The girls in the kitchen had the hot water urn on boil and the dozens of beautiful cakes spread out in display on our dining table. The variety of cakes was simply astounding, cheese and bacon muffins, millionaire's cake, sponge cakes, flapjacks. This list could go on until my account was as long as Lord of The Rings! The ladies of Campoverde had excelled themselves once again. And so, we managed setting it all up with minutes to spare before the 10am deadline. Then they arrived.

Christine Jackson and her friend were at the front gate, checking the tickets or taking five euros from those who simply turned up without one. They also ran the tombola stall with the aid of her husband Kevin. Shirley McGennity and her friend, Trish, along with Carol Steer ran the bric-a-brac stalls and Lorraine Connor, Beryl, Janine and I took care of the drinks and cakes. Kevin Leonard sold raffle tickets and was nominated as the auctioneer for later. Kevin prowled the grounds of our house and no one willingly evaded him. He carried one of the black buckets we'd purchased from the Chinese shop. Periodically, he would come to me with this bucket full of cash. The money was simply pouring in. Hundreds of euros at a time were taken from the bucket and hidden away upstairs. At one such exchange outside, the wind managed to blow into the garden and took a five euro note from Kev's hand. It blew over the neighbours' wall. We never did find it.

Everyone was having a really good time. People were sat with their friends, chatting away. They were returning to the kitchen for seconds and we still had enough cakes for them to be batched up and sold later as people went home. They simply couldn't believe that we had managed to get it all set up. Kevin Leonard and I ran the raffle, and then it was his turn to become the auctioneer. He was a natural. Wit and repartee and a knack of eking out every last euro from our guests, and we guesstimated that there were around 150 of them.

Shortly after 2pm, the final guest departed. Praise from everyone to everyone. The committee set about clearing up. The girls rescued cake papers from the pool, collected the paper plates, plastic spoon and forks and other rubbish. They cleaned up in the kitchen and washed the dozens of cups, trays, etc. The lads collapsed the tables, stacked the chairs and carried them across to the community centre for storage until collection Monday morning. By 3:30pm, we were done and set off to our "office", Portobellos. We had bloody well earned this drink or two. Beer and burgers all round!

I had taken a few minutes time during the tidying up to hide myself away in the bedroom and set about counting the proceeds. I kept this to myself until an appropriate pause in the conversation at the pub. I announced in a very quiet but extremely excitable voice that the Coffee and Cake morning had raised over 1,600 euros. Silence, gasps of disbelief and beaming smiles! I'm even getting wet eyes writing this now several months after the event. You meet some people in life that never let you down, take that extra step for you and are so much more than just friends. I will never have the words to fully express my gratitude.

Just as a footnote to this, the books and a few items of bric-a-brac that were left were donated to PADS, which is a local animal charity.

As Dave and I managed the walking football team and were responsible for buying balls, cones, kits and the like, we struck up a relationship with one of the managers of the local decathlon store. He was informed of our fundraising and purpose of the team. Ultimately, he was also made fully aware of our "Camino Adventure" and our need for equipment. We struck a deal with him, whereby we saw the items we wanted, placed them on order to him via email and he would try and get us discount from head office. As Dave and I saw fit to buy stock that was already fully discounted and probably end of line, we never saw a cent of discount.

For those contemplating the Camino, here are the items I bought and their cost.

A. Merrell Waterproof Walking Shoes. See below comments. 86 euros.
B. Quechua rucksack with waterproof cover and detachable "man bag". 109 euros.
C. Walking tops x2. Both short and long sleeved. 53 euros.
D. Merino Wool Walking socks x2. 15 euros.
E. Blister resistant socks, short x2. 15 euros.

F.   Quechua weatherproof coat with detachable thermal lining. 87 euros.

G.   Lightweight sleeping bag. 10 euros.

H.   One pair of Snow gaiters. 15 euros.

I.   One pair of long hiking trousers with detachable bottoms. 49 euros.

J.   Two pairs of Lycra cycling shorts without padding to stop chafing. 20 euros.

K.   XL Waterproof Poncho. 27 euros.

L.   Walking sticks, 10 euros.

Total: 516 euros (I told you it wasn't cheap!).

Above are listed the "main" items, however there were others, ie, nail clippers, Vaseline (behave!) and a first aid kit which included a foil blanket, plasters, rehydration sachets and bandages. The list goes on as long as you want it to but try if you can to include essential lavender oil you can get from any health shop. Application of a couple of drops of this oil dries out your blisters almost instantly. I only had two blisters during the whole of the Camino, but my lavender oil was shared with dozens of other sufferers.

The one final piece of advice regarding equipment was to keep it to an absolute minimum. Ten percent of your body weight or less, if possible. Dave and I decided to limit it all to 9 kilos or as near as we could get to it. Yep! You're all at it again with your mathematically genius minds. Dave and I must weigh 90 kilos or there about, that's 14st 2lb in old money, but I suspect it's a good few pounds more. Portly, yes, that's it, we are portly. How polite.

In preparing for such an undertaking you get advice and offers from a lot of well-meaning people.

Tom Walker, a long-term friend and experienced walker, suggested walking shoes, not boots, and the make Merrell. A good call. They were comfortable, lightweight and waterproof, and boy did I need the latter. I had read in support of this that many pilgrims suffer from shin splints due to wearing boots and often discard them in the early days, replacing them with shoes. The shoe recycling bins around Pamplona must be stuffed with them. My only observation, post Camino, regarding my choice of footwear, was that the tread seemed to wear out quite rapidly compared with the Decathlon "Quechua" walking shoes that Dave purchased. They did the job for him too and cost half the price of mine.

The waterproof coat was my best purchase. It was fantastic. Not a drop of water got through it, even though the first eight days were completed in torrential rain. Then there was the snow and blizzard up to Cruz de Ferro. I had detached its thermal lining, which I used as my "going out jacket", post daily trudge. I cannot fault it, really. It was that efficient the only downside was the fact that it created so much condensation inside that I was saturated from within which later caused a problem with my mobile phone!

Two friends who lived on the estate wanted to help. Donald McDonald offered to take us both training up some local mountains, proper ones not "bumps", and how I regret never taking him up on that offer. But maybe if I had, it would have put me off doing the Camino before I'd started.

Then there was Phil Thompson, not only a captain in the army but also a Camino veteran, having completed the Camino de Santiago on at least three occasions. His last one being around the same time Dave and I started training. He is fit as a flea and offered to have a meeting with us at his home before we departed.

Dave and I turned up at his villa and were escorted through to his study. There, on the wall, were his framed Camino passport and "Compostela Certificates". He told us that they meant more to him than his OBE that stood proudly alongside.

Phil turned to the matter in hand. He turned on his computer, loaded the scores of photos and off he went. Blimey, were we in for an eye-opening education. He impressed upon us the importance of weight. Only to take half a tube of toothpaste, half a bar of soap, a maximum of three of everything in the clothing department, and if you thought that two would do, then that's fine. One pair of shorts, one top, one pair of socks, one pair of underpants worn one day, washed and dried and ready for the cycle two days later. He told us to hang the clothes off our rucksack as we walked in order to dry them. We had some difficulty with that concept during the first eight days.

Every gram we carried would have an effect on our ability to walk the Camino. We thought he was obsessed but he knew best. Subsequently, a bar of soap was cut in half and I didn't take a new tube of toothpaste. I did, however, take my iPad as well as my iPhone which Phil baulked at. He said that I could do everything on my phone that I could on the iPad. Technically, he was right, but it was so much easier to type my intended daily blogs on the iPad. History has shown me that I was right. Had I not had my choice, contrary to Phil's advice, I would have lost contact with the outside world for nearly half our journey.

Phil also told us that even though we were departing in early April that whenever the sun shone, it would be mostly on our back and that we must protect our necks. Dave already had a cap with neck protector attached, so Phil kindly gave me his. Phil talked about washing our "bits" as often as possible. Not only in the showers and toilets of the Albergues but in any river and stream we may come across. He was obsessed with not getting infections that would bring the Camino experience to a halt. Maybe he was right and in the heat of summer, I can almost understand his point of view. As it happened, Dave and I showered at least once per day and also had a thorough wash on top of that. Thankfully, we didn't get any infections. Captain Phil had inspired us but also set in motion the daily routine of unpacking and repacking my rucksack in order to keep the weight down. He also gave some great advice regarding posting some of the equipment we no longer required, back home during the pilgrimage. Items like snow gaiters may be would be a consideration. Thankfully, it never came to that, as I managed to get the rucksack weighing in at a fraction over nine kilos. Almost one kilo of this was my heart/cholesterol medication, which would clearly reduce on a daily basis. Finally, I was happy with my kit, its weight and how it felt on my back. Three or four training days, fully loaded, before our departure would help my back, shoulders and legs acclimatise.

My son Dan and his wife Katie had already bought me another walking top by "Body Armour". Pauline and Ricardo bought me a pair of Marino wool socks as well. The other necessities I will detail later as I packed, unpacked and repacked many, many times before setting off.

I am a self-confessed "technophobe" and would be happier if I could use pigeons, slate and chalk, not that I ever have, but I'm sure you get my point. A five-year-old is far more technically advanced than I am. With this stumbling block in my way, I turned to yet another friend, Don Stuart, who was fearless in the face of gigabytes, downloads and other such wizardry. All I wanted was some of my favourite music downloading from my broken iPod onto my phone. My iPod had been a 50th birthday present off my lads which they'd had engraved. I can't throw it away, even though it's irreparably broken. Not only had they had it engraved, but they had downloaded around 70 albums onto it, none of which I could currently listen to.

Don took me to his "studio", where he managed to retrieve the albums I had selected and uploaded them onto my Apple iPhone 5s. Not all of them appeared but enough to keep my ears occupied. Cheers, DJ Don.

The days ticked by and I have to confess that my apprehension increased. Self-doubt appeared hourly and some deep soul searching took place in the last few days before the Camino began. Had Dave and I made the right decision? Had we done enough training (let me tell you here and now that the answer to that last question is, "No" but there again, I have realised that you cannot train hard enough for the Camino. You train en route)!

My minds "get out clause", when the self-doubt appeared, was to realise that 300,000 pilgrims completed the Camino de Santiago during 2017. I know that a good percentage only completed the last 115 kilometres from Sarria but some of the remainder were in their 70s or older. I'm 58, Dave's in his early 60s, and both seemingly in decent health. Surely, I/we would be okay?

And now the countdown started. Last training walk, healthy diet, lots of pasta and now the "Farewell Party" at Portobello Bar on Thursday, the 5th of April. This would not be a late night, well, not too late as a morning train from Murcia station to Pamplona awaited us just a few hours later.

Sadly, two days before the "Farewell Party" on Tuesday, the 3rd of April, there was some devastating news that put the whole Camino in doubt.

Janine had not been well for at least a couple of years. Memory loss, passing out, unable to concentrate. There were so many different aspects to her illness. I do not want to go into the ins and outs of this, nor will Janine let me, but it transpires that my wife had a tumour, sat on her pituitary gland inside her head. It is just beneath the brain and close to the optic nerves and is the control centre of a lot of your body's functions. Thankfully, on the upside, the tumour was thought to be benign. Janine convinced me that she would be alright and that we had enough friends to keep an eye on her. This was true, but still, what a decision! It's clear by my writing that I somewhat reluctantly walked the Camino. Even now, as I write in August 2018, she is still awaiting the operation to remove the tumour. I know that we could have postponed the walk but so much had been set in place, donated and was expected.

The final night before our departure had arrived. Posters had been put up weeks before the Farewell Bash and there was an element of excitement in the air.

Sensibly, we decided to have a good hearty meal at Portobellos before the evening truly went into party mode. We didn't intend to drink vast amounts but the food was a safety net to soak up any excess.

7 o'clock arrived and off we went. It was like a cork jettisoning from a champagne bottle.

First event was the "Head Shaving" that we promised everyone we would do to bolster the donations. Two lady hairdressers, Debbie and Maureen, turned up at Portobellos, complete with trimmers and gowns. The team members and the enthusiastic revellers crowded round outside as the first locks off Dave and me were shorn. I intuitively decided that the girls should leave a strip of hair over centre of our heads, Mohican style. Anyone wishing to pay could shave off the last locks. It raised a further 55 euros! There we were, almost bald and grinning like Cheshire Cats. Subsequently, Dave's hair grew back at a phenomenal rate and he'd had three haircuts before my next one some three months later.

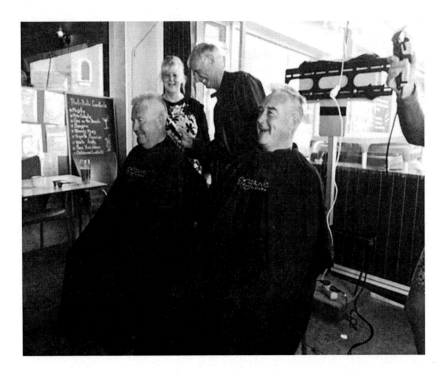

A friend of ours, Wayne Jackson, is a member of a Ukulele band, The Uke Club. They set the night off in fine style. They did a set for around an hour with their final number being "I Would Walk Five Hundred Miles" by the Proclaimers. They persuaded Dave and myself, wearing our sponsored T-shirts, to stand with them and sing along. There was no holding us. We belted out the lyrics, mostly without having to look down at the song sheets. The customers "were mad for it", as us Northerners would say. They were on their feet, stamping, clapping and dancing all over the pub. Scottish reels, dozy doing all over the place.

Most of the walking football squad were there too wearing their club polo shirts. Barry Wright, a reporter from a regional newspaper called The Costa Blanca News, was also there. We had met him earlier in the year, informed him of the team's charities, fundraising, and more importantly, he was aware of our Camino adventure. He took photos on the night and my daily blogs during the Camino would be sent to him via Debbie Coupe so he could prepare a weekly story in his paper. He was true to his word and what fantastic coverage he gave us. Even now, during August, he has covered our presentation of raised funds to the two charities. Thank you, Barry.

The final night was on fire. Post Uke Club, music was played and the celebration, dancing and drinking went on until around midnight, when, being sensible, we called it a night. The landlady, Louise, said that it was one of the best nights they'd ever had in the bar. Time for bed and a few hours' sleep. The train journey north was only a few short hours away.

Journey of Trepidation

Camino Blog – Friday 6th April 2018

A long and relatively boring day. Up at 6:30am, I said goodbye to my best friend and soulmate after taking him (Elmo) for a walk. A very quiet car journey then ensued in the company of my Camino buddy Dave, his wife Debbie, Kevin, our mate and chauffeur, and Janine. It was so silent in the car that I said I felt like a condemned man. A multitude of emotions swirled around the cabin of Kevin's car. I wouldn't say that I was scared but apprehension was seeping through my false smile and slightly clenched teeth. All of a sudden, we were at the entrance to the railway station in Murcia. I think the whole experience had affected everyone. It was quite a formal "au revoire", no tears or desperate hugs, just a brief squeeze, peck on the cheek and fond words. Dave and I had time to kill. No allocated platform yet for our train that was still some 45 minutes away. A quick check that all was okay in the ticket office and then time for a coffee, the type you only get in desperation. White plastic cup filled with brown liquid, whose identity is completely masked by a large dose of sugar. Further checks of the contents of our rucksacks ensued. Passports, check; phone and charger, check; train tickets, check.

I can speak some Spanish, but I understand more when listening to others. My ears soon latched on to a group containing several teenagers and their mothers standing close by on the platform. It transpired that they too were en route to Madrid. I engaged them in conversation just to confirm what I'd heard and knew we just had to get on the same train. Several minutes later, our train appeared and seemed to lumber, almost silently, up to us. Our tickets had a carriage and seat allocated. On to the right carriage, rucksacks stowed above, and Dave and I sat side by side, we were off. No going back now. The Camino and God knows what awaited us.

I had a window seat and stared out at the grey concrete of the city that passed by in silent reverence. This first part of the train journey was relatively uninspiring. The concrete turned to beige fields, rocky outcrops and undergrowth that in places seemed like it was trying to board the train. Small villages and towns floated by whilst Dave and I struck up stilted conversations clearly constricted by anxiety. We needed a few beers even at this time of day just to relax a little. No chance.

The train stopped at an unremarkable town. It remained stationary for an increasingly frustrating and anxious time. We had another train to catch in Madrid's Attocha station and this delay was putting that in jeopardy. Our adventure had barely begun, and we were being tested already. Finally, some 50 minutes later, we set off again. I went to the buffet carriage and spoke to a porter. He informed me that we would have to run through Attocha station to make the connection. Absolutely fabulous. Nine kilos and a coat on our back and running like cockroaches to a platform we knew not where.

Sadly, because of the delay, I was unable to take Dave to the section of Attocha station that is full of palm trees and greenery with bars and a terrace restaurant overlooking it. Many years ago, I had visited the station for a second time with two colleagues whilst working in Madrid. Ah! The delights of the drug squad. A visit on this day would have been a lovely start to our adventure had the time not evaporated.

Our train arrived at Attocha station and off we went like greyhounds from a trap. I suspect that should be cockroaches now I've mentioned them, but you get the picture. Up the lengthy ramps, stairs and skipping around other travellers, we arrived at a barrier and check point before access to the other platforms was gained.

We managed to board the train to Pamplona with minutes to spare. We left the urban sprawl of Madrid and out into the vast upper expanses of Spain. The grey clouds loomed, and the rain started to lash the windows of the train. Unbeknown to us, this was just a foretaste of what was ahead. The conversation between Dave and myself was punctuated with sighs as over eight hours on the train took its toll. Half an hour before Pamplona, a large mountain reared up to our left, its upper levels caked in snow. We gawped at it and our minds wandered far ahead. Really? Would we have to face climbing peaks like this?

We disembarked and jauntily stepped out of Pamplona station. Anyone could have stuck a bright, neon sign above our heads with one word shining brightly in the grey and wet gloom, "PILGRIMS!".

Dave had a Sat Nav on his mobile phone which was to prove invaluable in the next few weeks. First right and then left signal fading and then returning, 500 yards the wrong way. Sheltering in doorways from the rain, we finally managed to get a signal strong enough and that lasted long enough to evaluate our position. Got it! Up the hill, across a park and towards the centre of the city. Second left off the third roundabout and we would be there. Bollocks! We stopped at a kiosk, I spoke my best Spanish and looked at the blank faces staring back at us. They did, however, point to the brass scallop shells and yellow arrows painted on the pavement. They were all pointing in the wrong direction on this day. We would walk back this way some four days later.

Finally, around 7:15pm, we arrived at the Aloha Hostel. A friendly greeting from a young woman called Martha and a brief guided tour. The hostel was well worn but with a lovely friendly atmosphere. Bunk beds in communal dormitories, toilets much the same, I mean communal. Beverages and breakfast included; 15 euros. Nervously, we left our rucksacks on our beds which we identified as "ours" by laying our sleeping bags out. We took our valuables in our "man bags" and set out to explore the city in search of a meal, a cheap meal! After one or two incursions into some local restaurants (which were far too expensive for pilgrims), we found "La Comida". A bright and seemingly new restaurant/tapas bar in the San Antonio area. This is a cobbled area close to the town hall and church of the same name. We looked at the menu and simply couldn't decide. The waitress approached. She was young, attractive with long dark hair and an engaging smile. We wanted a cheap white wine and three tapas, but which ones? She offered to help and said that she would pick for us. We were pilgrims and had little money, definitely no gambas (prawns), which are one of the most expensive tapas on any menu. These facts were not lost on her and off she went to discuss the options with the chef. The food she ordered was unbelievably good! Tomato salad, costillas and aubergine. The two tomatoes had been boiled, skinned, chilled and were served with a sardine and onion salsa with rocket. Thumbs up for the first course. The ribs (costillas) fell apart and were served with mashed sweet potato, whilst the final course, the aubergine, had been charred, baked, peeled and was served on top of a healthy slice of goats cheese with dried, fried onions on top and lots of honey sauce. It was fabulous. All washed down with a cheeky white Navarra wine and served with bread. 26 euros in total! Bargain. Spirits lifted and very tired we went back to the hostel and after a short while, around 10pm, two weary pilgrims went to bed. Earplugs in, we tried to sleep. It's amazing how aware you become of each solitary noise made by others and yourselves in a strange place. Night night, sweet dreams.

Hello, Iris

Plans are changing daily. We had decided to walk through Pamplona on the return without stopping. We would try and walk a further 10 kilometres if possible, should we have the energy. That would be day three of the actual Camino.

Our sleep had been disturbed, to say the least, but what should I expect? Some heavy snoring had woken us at 05:10am. No matter how we tried, we couldn't get back off to sleep so up at 06:50am. Showered and light breakfast. One or two young pilgrims were up too. They just milled about and seemed as if they were settled in the hostel and would not be leaving for some considerable time. Dave and I had other plans. It was grey and wet outside. We are planning to see the Running Bull statue (as per Captain Phil's photos) and the cathedral before boarding the coach to San Juan Pied du Port around 2:30pm.

Unwittingly, we passed THE cathedral en route to the magnificent statue of the running bulls. I had consulted the street map as we wandered around the wet streets but clearly I thought there were two cathedrals! Really! How many cities have two cathedrals (Apart from Liverpool and Greater Manchester)? Anyway, post goose chase, we returned to THE cathedral to find they wanted to charge 5 euros for adults and 3 euros for pilgrims. As we weren't pilgrims yet, and had no pilgrim passport to produce, we reneged. In any event, Murcia Cathedral is far more imposing, beautiful and interesting but I wouldn't want to cause a regional, ecumenical fracas. I realise we may not have been in the pilgrim state of mind but there would be plenty more religious fish in the sea on our journey.

We found the bus station, consulted the man in the ticket office but unfortunately there's no earlier coach so we are killing time drinking copious amounts of coffee for the next three hours!

The coffee we drank was served by two Chinese ladies in their cafe. Beyond rice paper screens, towards the rear of the premises, a small Chinese restaurant was laid out. Time to kill and a lengthy journey ahead of us, we decided to have our lunch here. Big mistake! One crap Chinese meal later, we wandered out into the rain and across to the coach station. A lengthy wait then ensued before the coach pulled in. It was not, however, boring. Whilst waiting in line, we met and spoke with several Americans, I will try and recall them… Sue and Paul from Wisconsin, just walking the Camino as "friends" nudge nudge wink wink to a blind horse. Then there was John from Illinois, who was waiting to join his daughter tomorrow, Maggie from Texas and Kate from San Francisco. The latter were two young women, I would guess in their twenties, who would team up during the early days.

I have to say the route to San Juan Pied du Port was depressingly fearful. A road, the likes of which, I have never travelled on before. Steep and incredibly winding…and this is the easiest route back up to Roncesvalles the following day! A 25 kilometre climb awaited us. I say the "following day", as Dave and I had initially set our sights on a full day's rest and had not been intent on setting off until Monday the 9th. Like I said, plans change, and they would almost daily.

I don't think the constant heavy rain was making our view of the route any brighter, but seriously, never-ending switchbacks and "S" bends on a one in five incline with the odd pilgrim trudging along the roadside. Heads down, hoods up and apparently blissfully unaware of the coach careering towards them, on they went. How would they ever make the top of the climb and short descent into

Roncesvalles. It would be the middle of the blinking night before they arrived. Personally, I cannot express how intimidated I feel. I would have to conjure up something from deep inside to face this challenge.

Once in San Juan (abbreviated for convenience), we eventually found the passport office. Here we are, soaking wet and sat in front of a table with a Chinese girl, who told us to call her "Iris", to our right. Ah, moment of reverie here regarding the name Iris. My son Ben's favourite song from university, "Iris" by the Goo Goo Dolls and a cracking stag weekend for him in Hamburg with a dozen of his mates and elder brother, Dan.

We sat there transfixed as a lovely French gentleman informed us that the weather was bad, and snow was forecast on the mountain overnight. Whoopee! It transpired that "Iris" barely spoke English, well why would she as she is Chinese! My Cantonese was non-existent. All of us tried to help her understand and she smiled. She did not have accommodation booked. She was told to follow us to our Gite and book in there. She did and is now sharing a cosy dormitory with Dave, Jose from Brazil and myself. Lucky girl? We had noticed she only had a small rucksack, like a kid takes to school and we passed comment. She informed us that her luggage had gone missing and as I write, she is trawling the shops for some suitable Camino gear whilst we drink more wine.

I forget the name of the genial guy who owned the accommodation and booked us in, but he was full of advice. He was glad to see that Dave and I had chosen walking shoes instead of boots as the latter tend to give you split shins! Didn't I mention this earlier? Nice to get some reassurance though.

Dave and I trawled the sodden, cobbled streets, looking for the best meal option. Hallelujah! A lovely French bar with a restaurant at the back. Pilgrim's menu served in half an hour for 11 euros, wine included. Out of the downpour and time for another swift glass of wine, an aperitif, they call it in these parts. Other pilgrims ventured in, and soon the restaurant had a lovely "bon ami" atmosphere. You'd think I was fluent in French wouldn't you? I'll try and throw in the odd Bonet de Duche and Petis Pois, a la Del Boy, later on!

The rain had been with us all day and intensified as the evening went on. We crawled into our bunks. I was full of dread for the day ahead. There was snow forecast overnight which may make the Napoleon trail too treacherous to consider. We will see tomorrow.

Footnote…up at 1am, it's an age thing, and it's teeming down in Biblical proportions!

Up! Up! And Away!

April 8th. First day on the Camino.
San Juan Pied du Port to Roncesvalles 24k.

Well, let me tell you it can rain here! Awake and up at 6:30am. Still dark. Discussion which route resulted in us choosing the Valcarlos way. The Napoleon was too dangerous. 10cm of snow had fallen, according to the passport office and as far as they were concerned, this pass was closed. Just to explain that the Napoleon Way is a steadier climb but goes 400ft higher. It's a scenic route but today you ain't going to see nothing! The Valcarlos way is gentle for 12k and then one in five steep for 9k. This is the way we went. We made an early decision to stick to the roads as far as we could and did so for 14k. I have to mention "Iris" again at this point. She had been awake and waiting for us in the gloom of our dormitory this morning. In my humble opinion, she should not be going on the Camino at all or at least not until her lost luggage appears. She is completely unequipped for this. She wore jeans, not good; ankle socks, not good; patent leather booties, not good either – a lightweight red kagoul and a small rucksack. The latter two items she had purchased the evening before. We embraced her as fellow pilgrims and swore an oath that we would look after her. One way or another, we would complete day one, reputedly the hardest day of all, together.

We stood there on the cobbled street of San Juan Pied du Port, the rain streaming down our faces. Our route chosen, well there was no option really, off we went. Barely a few steps had been taken when other figures appeared in the gloom. Each and every one shrouded and bedraggled in their waterproof ponchos. Quick and steady footsteps approached from behind the three of us. We had barely turned 90 degrees when a gazelle bounded past us. For gazelle, please read a 6' 3" tall, 70+ year old white guy. He was wearing a vest, shorts, a small pack on his back, knee high sports socks, good trainers and a head torch.

'Morning,' he said as he bounded on up the cobbles.

Clearly, an experienced fell runner for most of his years in my opinion, but right here and now, he was completely bonkers. He disappeared into the gloom. We would see him on several more days, up to and including Estrella.

The road ahead climbed imperceptibly. We were making good time. Iris was still with us and seemed unphased. The kilometres were passing quickly in these early stages. Clearly, we were walking at over 5k per hour as the various landmarks passed by. Occasionally, we had to leave the road as the shells and yellow arrows took us along paths through the wooded mountainside. The paths were nothing more than torrents of water as it sought the easiest way down to join the raging, foaming river below us. We were still climbing but it simply didn't feel like it. Hundreds of meters through the trees and down to cross the river via ancient bridges the path would then veer sharply upwards with the last 50 meters completed by wooden steps that still held firm. Out into the road again, we would collect our breath and sat on the metal roadside barriers. Spookily enough, they are the same height as my bottom. A couple of minutes respite, gulps of water and I turned to look at Iris just to ensure she was alright to continue. I found her squatted on her haunches inspecting the small roadside flowers. She looked up, rivulets of rain running down her alabaster face. A small smile.

I merely said, 'Okay?'

The smile broadened and we waved her forward. The small town of Valcarlos came in view and the time had come to have a hot drink and a bite to eat. Ponchos and rucksacks deposited outside, we entered the cafe which has a mini market adjoining it. Other pilgrims were buying their breakfast, an assortment of cheeses, cured hams and baguettes. We settled for a hot coffee, tomatoes on toast and a piece of cake. The locals had started the log fire in the grate of a metal fire, which had a glass door. The warmth and homely glow made it a great temptation to take off our coats, but it was cold, and we were just as soaking wet beneath them, due to condensation, as we were on the outside. No, the coats were staying on. We simply didn't have the time to dry them off. Half an hour later, we were back on the road. The gradient was ever steepening and the bends in the tarmac became tighter. It was now around 10:30 in the morning, cars appeared on the road and the bells of a local church were peeling, calling the faithful out on this most miserable of days to genuflect at the whim of the priest. It was a little normality. The times when we had to leave the road were tortuous. The terrain was simply awful. Mud, torrents of water over our boots and a raging flow ten meters below, sweeping all before it. We were always glad to rejoin the road. There were few pilgrims on this route. Even though we stopped every few hundred meters, and these stops were becoming more frequent, I can only recall half a dozen or so in sight. Two of these were Paul and Sue from Wisconsin, who would leapfrog us at every stop. Everything was starting to take its toll. The constant rain, the gradient and being wet from sweat inside and rain outside was draining. We trudged on. The below picture is of Dave with the orange rucksack, Iris in a red poncho and another intrepid pilgrim.

We, suddenly, after 20 kilometres or so, had the opportunity to go off road again onto the Camino route. Far across the valley and through the mist and rain to our left, we could see another dark mountain looming up. It was covered in snow. It seemed to join our mountainside possibly half a mile away. I guessed that this was the Napoleon route, and we made the decision that leaving the road was the best bet. What a mistake! The terrain was dreadful and continued for around 3k. Fallen trees blocked our path and the deepening mud wanted to suck the sodden shoes from our feet. Dave was showing signs of fatigue. He didn't want to go on. It was written all over his face. I decided that this dreadful path was best conquered 50 meters at a time. From one tree to another. Whatever

Dave and the incredible Iris could manage. Anything to keep them going. Surely the top couldn't be far now?

I strode on, stopped, looked back and encouraged them best I could. Iris had started to lag behind. It was hard enough for me and I was reluctant to go back to her. She was back on her haunches, feet planted in the mud, head bowed and shaking from side to side. I bellowed words of encouragement at her. Her head rose and her eyes met my gaze. Her head shook. She'd had enough. Dave stepped up by my side and as we peered down at her, two pilgrims came up the path behind her. We continued to shout, and the pilgrims clearly saw our dilemma. They bent over and spoke to her. They pointed up at us and we waved in encouragement. She stirred, rose and started to put one weary foot in front of the other. We were getting really cold by now and turned to climb what transpired to be the last few hundred paces to the summit over 4,500 feet up in the sky. Not a bad "bump" for the first day. Dave found new life now the summit had been breached, although he later admitted wanting to give up at various points during that first day. Iris joined us and almost skipped down the last two kilometres to Roncesvalles with Dave. My right knee was shot, and I struggled downhill as I would for the rest of the Camino.

I did say to Dave on the way up, 'Dave, you know this St James Guy? He must have been a Nutter!' Or something very similar.

The Albergue at Roscenvalles is truly something and it came up to our weary feet quicker than we anticipated. Bunk beds for 200+, hot showers, helpful staff, laundry, evening meal and breakfast booked at two adjoining pubs for the Princely sum of 25.50 euros plus 3.5 euros in total for our sweaty, wet clothing to be washed and dried. As I write, we are now sat in a lovely pub, where we have had a couple of well-earned drinks, some tortilla and bread and are now drinking a really nice bottle of wine pre evening meal at 7pm. We have already booked into our lodgings tomorrow in Lasarasoanna, another 25k away. We will sleep well tonight!

THIS HAS BEEN A BLOODY HARD DAY, PROBABLY ONE OF THE MOST PHYSICALLY AND MENTALLY DEMANDING DAYS OF MY LIFE. THE WINE IS THANKFULLY EASING THE MEMORY.

Addendum... The meal for ten euros was lovely. Veg soup, pasta, chicken and chips, ice cream with more WINE and water. It soon became apparent whilst talking to our Camino buddies during the evening meal that many of them, some we had talked to on Saturday evening, had chanced going over the Napoleon pass, contrary to the advice of the passport office. They shared photos from their phones and cameras, which showed lines of footprints in the snow, which disappeared into the dense cloud and mist. They all admitted that they had "chanced it". We later found out that the week before we had set off, two Irish guys had ignored the advice from the passport office and attempted the Napoleon Pass. They had not made it and had to be airlifted off the mountain. It cost them 10,000 euros each. Truth or fiction, it's clear that the passport office's word is the law. Ignore it at your peril, any would-be renegades!

It is now twilight and most pilgrims are settling for the night. We have two lovely bunk bed amigos, Frank and Annetta from Denmark and Germany, respectively.

This Camino is amazing! Americans, Canadians, Chinese, Japanese, Spanish, German, Paula from Italy, South Africans, New Zealanders. And it has to be said each and every one are the kind of people you would love as your neighbour!

Sweet dreams, world, and may peace be with you.

Pilgrim Albergue at Roncesvalles. No standing on parade here!

False Sense of Security

Day Two. Roncesvalles to Larrasaona. It says 28k? GPS says 31+

We set off in high spirits! Coffee and toast first and then immediately off to a sign across the road for the popular photo opportunity, where the sign says 790k to Santiago.

The first few kilometres of the day were flat but wet and muddy. No change there, then! It was cold, only one degree but we soon warmed up. The sun came up and shone, as the forecast predicted…until 12:30pm! After a few kilometres, the hills rose to the right, some with snow on. Someone, God bless you, as you made me smile, had placed thousands of stones to make three letters, probably three meters in height, on the hillside. It simply read "SOS", ah the Camino sense of humour. I had, in fact, seen this two days before when being taken by coach the other way.

We made the most of the warmth as we walked through villages which seemed distinctly French in design and then through farmyards and into the countryside.

We then encountered some steep ascents, not too long, maybe 1k or a little more but by the heck they were testing this early on. Partway up one of them, shortly after a mid-morning coffee break, a young pilgrim came up behind us. He can't have been 20. He was from Northern Italy, skinny with a haunted look about him. We said 'Hello' and had a brief conversation with him. He was called Hercules. How appropriate we thought. Almost all of our conversations at this point of our journey started off wanting to know "WHY?" Hercules informed us that he had come on the Camino to 'sort some things out in his mind.' We didn't like asking any more questions, too soon. We all smiled and on he went. We haven't seen him since.

As we continued up the climb, I looked across the valley and saw what I thought were nine eagles circling half a kilometre away. They were difficult to distinguish and I have now concluded they were in fact vultures. That having been said, some 500 meters further on, we went over a crest, woods in a valley to our left, and a solitary golden eagle taking to the air. No mistake here, it was a magnificent sight, barely 200 meters away. Right at that moment, I wished I was that eagle, it would have been so much easier to soar above the Camino whilst secretly smirking at the pilgrim's trials and tribulations.

The day simply became harder, and in truth, was just as difficult as day one but for different reasons. Yesterday, we were mentally prepared for a hard day whilst today all the information said how easy it would be, as well as all downhill. Simply not the truth. We had been lulled into a false sense of security.

The terrain was nothing but mud and soaking wet stones all being washed down in the constant new torrents of water. It was horrendous. Dave and I had started to open up to each other. Yes, we were mates, but we knew nothing about each other's past and family. The deaths of our fathers, the impact each traumatic episode had on our lives, our sons, their development, the death of Dave's first wife, mother and my divorce were all brought out into the daylight beneath the sodden trees. As sad and as poignant that this was, I realised that we were bonding.

We had reached the top of this particular mountain and the ground levelled out beneath our feet as we trudged through the forest. Up ahead of us was a Goliath of a man. He was at least six foot six inches tall, as broad as a small tree and with long wavy hair and full, bushy beard. He was ruddy faced and had steely, determined eyes. In his right hand, he dragged behind him what can only be described as an elderly ladies, large shopping trolley, the rectangular, tartan one with the two wheels and a stand, you know the one I mean. The difference was that this one was covered by a bright yellow plastic sheet and had a number of ropes wrapped around its handle.

In his left hand, a sturdy, 30 foot of rope stretched out before him. At its end was a lean, Belgian Shepherd dog, sniffing around the undergrowth and leaf mould. What an impressive sight they made. Dave and I were instantly and completely in awe of this giant of a man. How the hell was he managing the trolley and dog whilst dragging himself and them, through the mud and stone ruts in this bloody awful weather? Oh yes, it was raining again.

As with every other pilgrim, we said, 'Buen Camino.'

He smiled and replied the same.

Later, we established his name was George, and a little more about him but that can wait.

Then the descent was upon us, and what a tortuous hour or so we were about to encounter. All I have to say is that the descent was intense, steep and dangerous. The loose stones gave way under our feet, the ground fell away in a very steep gradient and the rocks that were proud of the soil were stacked in a way that they resemble clumps of slates on their ends. Houses appeared through the trees at the base and the path levelled out to meander through the trees. Time to catch our breath. Dave consulted his GPS app on his mobile phone as he would do a dozen times a day. We had to press on to Zubiri. This was our next sanctuary where we would take lunch.

The cafe here was modern and warm just on the other side of a river which we crossed via a bridge. The river is the river Arga and the gothic bridge is called the Bridge of Rabies. Mmmmm lovely. Local folklore would have you believe that in the distant past, the farmers would drive their livestock over the bridge, around its central pillar three times in order to rid them or prevent them from getting Rabies.

Wisconsin Paul and Sue joined us in the café, and we all ate heartily. Too heartily in my case. I was hungry and stuffed myself with an assortment of treats. Note to self and other prospective pilgrims, eat light and drink plenty or you will struggle shortly after as I did on this day. As we huddled in the café, the heavens opened yet again. We ventured out, and as we donned our rucksacks, followed by our ponchos, we saw George, his dog and trolley cross the bridge. One word, WOW!

At this point, I noted to myself that both Paul and Sue both wore bright yellow ponchos, and as they pottered off into the distance, I christened them "The Minions". It amused me for some kilometres as I glimpsed them between the trees ahead. Several pilgrims would be christened with names appropriate to their behaviour or dress sense during the next month.

Off we went, back across the bridge and turned right, running parallel with the river. A pleasant walk out of Zubiri spoilt by large industrial monstrosities. Corrugated metal industrial buildings in grey or green. Nothing too inspiring. Five and a half kilometres further on was Larrasoana and our refuge for the night. It seemed much further. En route, we reached a point on the path where a stream going downhill and directly across had flooded our way. A lady who was walking her dog was on the other side some four or five meters away. She had thrown some quite large branches and poles into a clump just our side of halfway. How they remained there, I will never know. Jumping across this impasse normally would be a hard ask but with a nine-kilo rucksack on your back and another two kilos of water dragging you down it seemed so daunting. Head down, arse up and into the air I leapt. One foot aimed and planted on the largest branch, I hit the raft. Water swamped over my shoes but that was it and I cleared to the other side. Dave followed and we said a great big "thank you" to the unknown woman, although her little dog was none too happy at these two large figures descending on its owner. Wet feet, that was all, it could have been much worse if we'd gone apex over tip.

Larrasoana appeared between the trees and like magic, the rain stopped and the sun shone. It was welcome but personally I reached the Albergue dejected, soaked and in some pain. I stripped off, well almost, and collapsed on the bed. Dave fared much better and was first in the shower. My right knee was swollen and very sore. Time for the Ibuprofen cream, anti-inflammatory and paracetamol tablets. These were becoming part of my staple diet.

Not much going on in Larrasoana but at least they have a bar! Just another source of pain relief.

Well, what an interesting evening was had in a tiny hamlet where the chickens find it difficult to occupy themselves. We sat alone for a while in the only bar. It had a welcoming log fire burning and two female bar staff, who seemed pleased to see maybe the first two pilgrims of the season. We were subsequently joined by Alma from Iceland, Julius and his friend Ritchie from Germany, a lady from Denmark called Rosa, a guy from Denmark we see every day called Nicholas and then there was Lloyd from Cornwall. The wine flowed and we laughed until 10pm, apart from when Julius showed us his swollen knee. It was far worse than mine. We thoroughly enjoyed each other's company. It was a brilliant night. We had met some kindred spirits whom we would see often over the coming weeks. It was also a good job our beds were less than 50 meters away and somehow the pain in my right knee didn't seem too bad!

Wet Hugs and High Fives

Day Three. Larrasoana to Zariquiegui via Pamplona, (again).27k.

We had decided to get going by 8 am. I can't imagine why we needed an extra half hour in bed but wish it had been half a day. Raining again, cold, only 5 degrees but with the wind lashing at our ponchos, it felt much colder. From early on, we were followed almost continuously by a red kite. Even in this miserable weather, it was out looking for its breakfast. It was lovely to watch as it conquered the wind, constantly twitching its tail and wings. As they feed on carrion, maybe he had a beady eye set on the hobbling man from Manchester.

Two early climbs and then the terrain flattened out but once again so much mud and water. It's really difficult to keep your feet dry. Everyone was struggling. More pilgrims seemed to be on the road/path today. At times, we would form a crocodile some twelve or so people long. This did nothing for the treacherous footing as our shoes were submerged in the brown ooze. A couple of hours walk short of Pamplona a pilgrim from a previous pilgrimage had set up his own coffee stop in the middle of nowhere. Half a dozen of us hunkered down in this incomplete, cement cowshed whist he brewed coffee "cowboy style" in a billy can on a camping stove. It was very welcome. He offered bread, cakes, water, trinkets and all sorts of stuff that was laid out on a wall. No prices, just a donation.

We pushed on and eventually entered the suburbs of Pamplona. We stopped on a bridge over the river Ultzama. It was a raging torrent, just a foretaste of what was ahead in the coming week.

Dave stopped in a shoe shop, where he purchased some comfy shoes for our evenings out and I dived into a chemist for more anti-inflammatory tablets. Lloyd from Cornwall joined us. He was limping along, having problems with his right foot. He was also wearing shorts and a T-shirt! They make them tough and stupid in Cornwall. It was bloody freezing. A few kilometres later, Dave stopped, checked his rucksack and sighed. He'd left his metal flask of cool water in the shoe shop. I offered to wait whilst he walked back or caught a bus. No, sod it. It was gone. Plastic bottles would do in future. Not that we would constantly buy them but merely top up two each at every opportunity.

We truly entered Pamplona via an historic rampart and through what appeared to be the city walls. Wet cobbles underfoot, we found ourselves outside the city hall. Time for lunch. Tapas and a coke. Another pilgrim joined us as we sat at a table in the window of the cafe and watched citizens, tourists and pilgrims scurry by. The young lad ordered a hearty pilgrim's menu. He was South Korean and had a camera strung around his neck. For the previous two days, he seemed to stop every 30 meters and take a photo of whatever intrigued him. I'm surprised he'd kept up with us. Nickname time, I shall call him Mr Nikon, although other makes of camera are readily available.

Replete, we pushed on through the city, our heads folded to the pavement searching for every brass scallop shell and yellow arrow. We came across the cabin, where three days previously, we had sought directions to our hostel. This time, the arrows went in the right direction. As we reached the far side of Pamplona, the weather turned for the worse. It went distinctly cold and the rain teemed down. We took temporary shelter in a bus stop. Our destination, Zariquiegui, was still nine kilometres away.

We arrived at our Albergue, which was not an inspiring resting place. It was freezing cold inside. Zariquiegui is a one-horse town on the side of a mountain. Dave has succumbed to a blister, which we will sort out with the essential lavender oil I've brought. It's simply magic, drying the blister out almost instantly. Showered and rested, we are in the bar of the Albergue but drinking hot chocolate and tea! I had entered the bar sometime after Dave as I've decided to have a nap and get warm on my top bunk. He was agitated by something. His lips were tight and thin, and he took my gaze. He inclined his head to his right, and I followed it. Two tables away, an oldish guy with a thick Irish accent was talking to a younger woman. It transpires that the Irish guy had engaged Dave in conversation before my arrival. He had told Dave that he hated the British, the police and God knows what else. He was a Republican from a bygone era and seemingly didn't give a toss who he upset. I know Dave well enough to say that he definitely would never have disclosed being in the police, but his accent clearly gave him away as being British. Dave was just being friendly but now his hackles were right up as he tipped me off to avoid this individual. The Irish relic was on his third Camino. Apparently, his wife didn't mind. I can't imagine why!

Dave and I are just two simple human beings, making our way through the Camino, whilst raising money for charity. Thankfully, this bloke was unique as far as our experiences went.

To lighten the mood, Ritchie, our new, young German friend has just walked through the door, which reminds me of a saloon bar in a western movie. Not that it swings to and fro, but everyone looks round and stares at the stranger entering town. Ritchie was sodden. His glasses steamed up but let out a loud shout of 'Ya' when he saw us. Big wet hugs and high fives all round. Sadly, he told us that Julius had stayed in Pamplona, as his knee had swollen even more, then had turned blue and green. His Camino was over. He was catching a plane back to Germany tomorrow.

This bloody Camino does get to you in ways I never imagined. Dave has been brilliant. He is taking care of me like a big brother. Scrunched up newspaper in my shoes two evenings on the trot and constant support and attention. One of life's great guys. Bromance? No, but we will see each other through this.

Every day two things are paramount, finding newspaper at the Albergue to stuff in your sodden boots to help dry them out and Wi-Fi at every stop be it a cafe or Albergue.

Footnote, I used walking poles today for the first time due to my knee. I'm still not sure if they achieve anything. More practice needed. The constant "tap, tap, tap" really got on my nerves.

The Viper's Nest
and Other Expletives

Day Four. Zariquiegui to Lorca. 30.36k.

Well, you've all heard of the "roaring forties", well, last night in our dormitory of eight, it was the "Snoring Forties". Not a lot of sleep but up before dawn and on the road towards Lorca just before 8am. The first 45 minutes were all uphill to a crest with a well-known Camino monument on top. It's a series of metal pilgrims and donkeys. We took videos at the top but could hardly make ourselves understood as we sent greetings to anyone who cared to listen. The wind was absolutely howling, and the wind turbines were happily whirring away.

It was all downhill from here but the first 2k were severe. A pebble strewn path with more torrents of running water. We took our time! One pilgrim was in a rush. The guy who jogged past us at the start of day one, "Charlie Hot Feet", who we had decided was a fell runner simply bounded downhill without a care for the uneven and loose rocks. A courtesy nod and raise of a hand as he went on regardless. Quite remarkable. Some lovely little villages, a coffee and tostadas in Uterga some 6k along the road. But now it's head down and off again with the rain and wind easing.

On to Puente la Reina via Muruzabal and Obanos.

Puente la Reina was lovely. Century-old churches with Storks nesting on top. Narrow historic streets with a fabulous café where we stopped for lunch. Six gorgeous tapas between us for ten euros, bargain! Well fed and watered and ready for the afternoon.

Dave at the start of Puente la Reina, poncho still on

Time for a little moan here. It was now early afternoon and a chill wind took any of the warmth provided by a watery sun. We were tired and approached a little town called Cirauqui. A well placed bench was found tucked away out of the wind in the first extremities of this small town and we made the most of our five-minute break by taking on some water and warming ourselves in the faint, tepid, rays. Now, Cirauqui can only be described as a collection of buildings stuck on a tiny hill, which is in the shape of a Christmas pudding. The path that lay ahead took us left and right so many times and up steeply to the zenith of the town, where you guessed it, there was another church. Blimey Charlie, thereafter, wouldn't you know it we descended steeply to the far side of town through more narrow winding streets. Why the hell doesn't the Camino simply take you around the flat outskirts? Ah, sorry, I almost forgot…this is a spiritual and religious adventure!

Research shows that "Cirauqui", in Basque, means "Vipers Nest". I have to admit that upon leaving Cirauqui, I felt like one of them had well and truly bitten us both on the arse.

For a few minutes, we struggled to find the yellow arrows to take us back on the Camino. Dave found the only person out and about in Cirauqui, a bloke repairing a roof. He pointed in the direction of the main road a few hundred yards away. Off we went, picked up the arrows and crossed the main N110 and A12 into the countryside.

Did I mention how tired we were? I'm sure I did. Straight in front of us lay a gentle, stony, path which rose gently and inviting. Spirits lifted, we took the first few steps, only to see one of our guiding arrows point left, around a corner and onto a rocky path that rose so steeply in front of us that I left out a stream of expletives. It started with "bloody", then there was an "F", the mention of a sea bird beginning with "S", the dreadful "C" word and finally "Bollocks". Dave burst out laughing, bent over, placed his hands on his knees and belly laughed. He managed to splutter that he had never heard that phrase before, but it would stick in his memory. It would make him smile on a number of occasions during the coming weeks.

We pressed on. A few kilometres before our night stop in Lorca, we saw one or two vultures to our right and then above us. Wheeling round and round as they rode the thermals, which I'm surprised exist due to the weather. Anyway, one or two became a couple of dozen, this became over 40 until finally we estimated at least 60 of these magnificent birds above and to our right.

God, I wish my granddad was here to see this!

Then there was a mirage only one kilometre further. A bright yellow bar umbrella in an area full of piles of pilgrim stones, rickety old benches and a table with fruit, water, cans of beer and fruit juice on. There was an offering tin amongst the goodies. A young guy appeared from amongst the olive trees and engaged us in conversation. He was trying to clean and "improve" this little oasis before the full flood of pilgrims washed over him in coming months. He had no chance with the mud, mud and more mud. I, as I am prone to doing, Christened it, "a Nepalese, hippy, refuge". It even had those sacred, good luck bunting streamers you see at the Everest base camp and all around the Himalayas.

This one photo doesn't do it justice!

Albergue de Lorca in less than one hour. Our host was a lovely man called Jose Ramon. Water placed in front of us as soon as we entered. It had been a long day.

We were escorted around the end of the bar as the wind picked up outside. The blue, corrugated, metal delivery door at the front rattled as we passed. The stairs to our dormitory rose to our left. Many sets of muddied boots, stuffed with newspaper lined the steps and ours joined them, rather than traipsing mud through the stone upper corridors.

Showered, refreshed and down to the dining area/bar late afternoon. It was now howling a freezing gale outside. We were joined by a "new pilgrim" to us. A bloke in his 40s called Dee from Scotland. Then in came Joe from Hawaii, Nicholas from Sweden, Rosa from Denmark, Bride and Ritchie from Germany. "The Party Group" almost complete, except for 20-year-old Julius, who sadly flew home from Pamplona to Germany with a bad knee yesterday. And then a woman called Liz appeared. She was 30, blonde and from South Africa. Via wine and good conversation, we found out that she had ran a number of "boot camps" as a business. She had given them up and come to the Camino to find herself. She was on her own. Both Dave and I immediately took to her and held her under our collective wings. Liz would surface periodically from here on. It was another good evening. Ritchie, God bless him, must have won the pools (for those who remember them) or the lottery, as speculators now gamble on. He kept disappearing to the bar and returning with a number of bottles of house red wine. Dave and I treated the group to a round too. The others merely enjoyed themselves.

Going back to Dee, he was quite a strange guy. An air of solitude hung around him. He was walking the Camino in an unhurried fashion, say five kilometres per day. All he seemed to be interested in were Thai massage parlours. I'll let you make your own minds up!

Liz and Ritchie managed to use the old computer in the bar and it played some of our favourite music by request, as they became our resident DJ's. Jose Ramon merely leant on the bar, smiling as his takings increased by the minute.

Led Zep, The Sex Pistols, Alt-J, Deep Purple, Deacon Blue and finished the evening with a rousing sing along to Oasis before our host sent us to bed, all suitably refreshed. Oh, and Liz had introduced us all to a group called Mango Groove too. Dave approved.

A milestone today, over 100k, in fact 120k in total.

Meditation, Scriptures or One Last Beer?

Day Five. Lorca to Villamayor de Monjardin. (19k).

Up at 7:10am, the morning routine is well and truly setting in. Out before 8am and into the rain towards Villamayor de Monjardin via Villatuerta, Estella, Ayegui and Azqueta.

A relatively short day today, only 19.36k. However, the last eight are all uphill, and blinking heck, do I mean uphill!

Two kilometres before Estella, we walked through a concrete subway and out onto a tree lined bank some 50 meters above a huge raging river. The river Ega. Two or three other pilgrims milled about close by, uncertain what to do due to the unfolding events below. Dave and I gazed at the foaming torrent. Our path weaved down to the river, where a bridge would normally have taken us safely to the other side. A further group of six or so pilgrims were below us, clearly debating the bridge issue. It was under several feet of water at both sides. They returned up the muddy trail to us and said it was too dangerous. However, we watched in disbelief as a Spanish girl took off her boots and socks, rolled up her trousers and waded in. She held her rucksack above her head. She must have been crazy. Over knee deep in a raging flood without knowing what was underfoot. She made it to the first part of the bridge, and we breathed a collective sigh. Over she went and then down into the flow once again. Maybe three to five meters left through the river. Thank God she made it. I will never ever understand what possessed her to take such a risk, but we turned tail and went to the road.

It was only a 20-minute walk into Estella and we finally arrived at a bridge that hadn't succumbed to the river. It delivered us back onto the trail. Dave found his legs today. I lagged behind a little. I wish I'd found mine! In Estella, Charlie Hot Feet, the elderly fell runner, passed us. We were not to see him again and sincerely hope he completed whatever was his goal.

On dry land again across the bridge and into Estella.

The 8k up from Estella to Monjardin was tough and we arrived there together, but this was only after we visited the famous wine fountain. The fountain is to be found on the outer wall of a monastery (Santa Maria la Real de Irache) in Irache, where they brew wine. The monks provide 100 litres per day "gratis". There is an alternative tap for water! Six of us arrived together. Obligatory photos and somebody produced a cup, filled it and passed it around. Thankfully, I was last. Following the comments from the others who found it atrocious, I reneged. In any event, I'd had enough the previous evening, courtesy of Ritchie.

During the last couple of kilometres, the sun peered through the grey mass and the welcome warmth enveloped us. By the time we reached Villamayor de

Monjardin, it was really pleasant, and we were set to enjoy some of the best views on the Camino and spend a nice afternoon in the company of some lovely people. The Albergue we had booked is in Villamayor de Monjardin and is over 400 years old. It is reputed to have one of the best views from an Albergue on the Camino. It didn't disappoint.

We had to wait until 2pm to book in. Free coffee and tea was provided in a "do it yourself" reception area, where we took our boots off and stuffed them with newspaper, placing them on a rack until the morning.

Sun through the clouds at last. It was warm and very welcome. We enjoyed a quiet afternoon. Everyone rushed to get their sodden clothes out on the wall mounted maidens, which were becoming cram packed. Paul and Sue (minions), along with South African Liz, arrived.

After a relatively lazy afternoon basking in the warm sun, we had a lovely pilgrim dinner with 30 other Peregrinos. It is a Christian hostel. Pictures of Christ, crucifixes all over the dining room. We said prayers beforehand. Our hosts were three young American girls, who have applied all over the world to work in such religious refuges. They offered meditation and reading from the scriptures at 8:30pm but we preferred a last beer in the bar next door, heathen sods!

Point of interest… The King of Pamplona, Sanchez Garces, who reigned from 905 until 925 was buried in a monastery several hundred feet above our Albergue. No, I'm not climbing another bloody hill to see another relic, not today at any rate. Early to bed now as a long day lies ahead. Our room certainly was 400 years old. No heating, just extra horse blankets. Bare wooden beams in the ceiling and creaky floors. A wavy and uneven staircase with a closet that doubled as a shower at the top. Humble and basic but we were now enjoying everything that the Camino threw at us.

The minions to my left in some more bright colours.

King Sancho Garces.

Above is a poster from the bar we visited post evening meal. The top two pictures within show the monastery several hundred feet above us. The bottom two pictures are of a Roman baths, just a kilometre away, which we passed en route into Villamayor de Monjardin. Two German lads apparently went skinny dipping in the freezing cold natural waters that run from the hillside into the deep pool. One of them is in the green-coloured "Crock" shoes in the previous group photo. He reportedly wore these "Crock" shoes for many kilometres as his boots had been ditched.

And You Call This "A Fight"?

Day Six. Villamayor de Monjardin to Viana. (31k).

Good morning, pilgrims! The rain in Spain falls mainly on Dave and Steve.

Yep, more rain, more mud and a long day ahead. Up quite early. Coffee and out onto the Camino at 07:25am. It's barely light. A strange day really. Just trudging on. There's not a lot to see with your head down, keeping the rain out. Low cloud and not much fun. Head down arse up as they say. We are taking in the delights of Los Argos at breakfast. A lovely old historic town. Narrow streets and friendly people. Cup of tea, toasted sandwich and press on. The rain ceased, the clouds lifted, a little and the odd ray of sunshine peeped through the grey, leaden sky, as we entered Sansol and Torres Del Rio. The latter being made famous in the film "The Way", where the actors/pilgrims book into a Albergue, hosted by a man who can only be described as "eccentric". He held conversations with himself, as if somebody else was in the room.

The two villages were side by side with competing church bells regarding the current time. It happened to be 12:00pm as we walked between them. One striking a minute later than the other. There must be a time zone line around here somewhere! A welcome shop appeared, which had a small Albergue above it. The shop assistant was mopping the floor. I was chased into a small veranda with a table and chair. A can of pop, Kit-Kat and continue up and down, these bloody sharp and steep inclines. Just before I left the shop, a pilgrim in a kilt entered. Following a brief conversation, I found out that he had left his two companions, one a "Mountie" police officer from Canada. My fellow pilgrim had succumbed to a stomach bug and had just booked a room above the shop, where he planned to stay for a couple of days rest.

They hide these steep inclines around every blinking corner. Just when you see your point of destination a few kilometres away with a path leading you straight to it, off you go. 90 degrees right or left. Down a one in four and up a one in three. Never mind St James, this Camino was part of the Spanish

Inquisition! The air was blue at times. After a while, we crested yet another hill to be confronted by mounds of stones, some over a meter high previously piled up by pilgrims. I'd dread to place a little stone on the top of one and watch it crumble. All those hang ups, prayers, etc, at my feet.

Weather update…this is the worst weather in this region since the 1980s. The Ebro has flooded millions of hectares of land, animals, by their hundreds have drowned in the flooded fields and guess where we head for tomorrow?

Hell, we must have some penitence to cleanse from our souls.

Just to top it all off, 3k from Viana the rain swept in again from our left. Hoods back on, and I start to think of the hot shower 40 minutes ahead. The Albergue Izar is modern inside and has clearly been recently renovated. The showers, oh God, the showers. So hot, so powerful. They massage your aching back, limbs and whatever else you feel like. Off out now to sample the delights of this town. The centre is incredibly historic, as they all seem to be here, but the outskirts as we entered, reminded us of some Eastern Block suburbs from the 60s. Lots and lots of tenements. We settled in a cafe ran by an oriental lady. Two beers, watch the Spanish News, gawp at the flooded upper regions of the country and then we moved to a cafe/bar next door. The tapas in here were fabulous with plenty of variety. They were all laid out in the chilled, glass cabinets on top of the lengthy counter. We had several. Two lady pilgrims of a certain age entered and engaged us in conversation. They were from Australia. Sorry girls, but I have forgotten your names. They were very pleasant and became really interested in our "charitable" adventure.

Two burly Irish lads also entered the bar. They didn't stay too long, as they had been told there was an Irish bar in the town. Isn't there one in every city and town of the world? They left on a mission to find this particular one. They had, however, been "had over". No Irish bar, just a fruitless amble through the damp cobbled streets for the rest of the evening.

Eventually, Dave and I decided to make our way back towards the Albergue but chanced one last drink in a typical Spanish bar around the corner. Drinks ordered, we sat at a table with a view to the large TV screen to which everyone's attention seemed to be fixed. A live bull fight was being screened. I'm sorry, but to call it a "fight" is a blatant lie. It's the one-sided torture of a truly magnificent animal whose only purpose in this world is to die, exhausted and skewered to death in front of a baying crowd. I know there are other blood sports, hare coursing, fox/stag hunting, so on and so forth, but I have to admit to being physically sickened by the events unfolding in front of me. My eyes were wet, and I was in a rage. Get me out of here before I throw something at the screen and end up fighting with the locals, who were clearly impressed by the chief tormentor in his tight trousers and glittering, short jacket.

I know it's historic, traditional and some people clearly enjoy it but if I never see these images again, it will still be too soon for me. I'm glad it's bedtime.

Dave doing the modelling tonight in Viana.

Update on Day Six.

Ten yards across the way from our tapas bar was the entrance to a church.

Once back to our Albergue, we met some pilgrims we knew, ie Nicholas and Lesley, who were cooking so we had one final beer from the fridge, just to be sociable. We have decided that tomorrow we are cooking…let's see!

Looking Back in Anger

Day Seven. Camino. Viana to Navarette. (22k)

Well hello, bloggers. We set off at 07:35am today. NO RAIN. Leaving Viana behind, we set off into the countryside. Still lots of mud and small raging torrents everywhere. We had walked five kilometres when we came to a bridge across a road. Full of high spirits, we bounded up to the top and turned to our right. There it was, straight in front of us. We couldn't believe our eyes. Less than two kilometres away with an arrow straight road leading us back to it was Viana. Dave said something I could not possibly repeat in this blog. We'd done five kilometres to make less than two via tarmac! Flipping heck! Not much else of significance until we approached Lograno. A little old lady with her stall of trinkets and Camino memorabilia on the descent into the suburbs. She insisted on stamping our pilgrim passports and a few cents were exchanged. Dave bought a trinket for his wife Debbie. As we entered the city, the river Ebro was in full flow. It was an impressive sight.

Onwards and into the city, which was dominated by two impressive cathedral spires. Unfortunately, the Camino path took us to the right of them. We stopped for coffee and light snack but decided to walk back a few hundred meters to see the cathedral spires, which had been so impressive from a distance. Wow, what a disappointment! Completely "uninspiring". No pun intended.

A long trek out of the city ensued, the only thing worth reporting, my saving of a damsel in distress. The man-made walkway out of town was full of people walking, jogging and cycling as they headed out and passed us and into what seemed to be a country park. One such Spaniard was a teenage female on a mountain bike. Not a care in the world, on the path, on the grass, anywhere she wanted until 50 meters ahead, she came to an abrupt halt. She dropped the bike, as if it had been plugged into the mains and walked around until she found a small stick. She then proceeded to pick up the bike, held it at arm's length and began to poke and prod something below the handlebars. As I approached, I was intrigued. I rode up on my white steed, well, I hobbled up, said 'Perdon,' and promptly removed the offending worm from where it had landed on the front of the bike with my fingers. A big smile, on she got and rode off into the distance.

Into Navarrete

A beautiful, historic town, whose streets run around the church in concentric circles. We booked into a lovely Albergue called Buen Camino. This was the view from our room of eight bunk beds.

This was the interior…no, not of our dorm!

See, it's not all beer and skittles.

I visited the church during the day and had a deep conversation with the big fella upstairs. I was alone when I did this and felt brave enough to speak out loud. Quite unburdening in a weird way, as I am still at an impasse in my life re the existence of God. Maybe I'll be wiser and have all the answers in four weeks' time?

Back to reality… 50 yards from the entrance to the Church of Navarette was a bar. It was a bar that both Dave and I wish we could find in every stop of the

Camino. A friendly, portly, landlord greeted us from behind a bar, which was laden with an assortment of fresh tapas. It was a sight for sore eyes.

Sun out, beer in hand, we settled for a couple of hours, before I ventured back to the Albergue and cooked our meal for the first time. Jamon and cheese for starters, pasta with salmon, peas, veg and white sauce with bread, followed by Creme Brûlée! Not bad hey? Well, pilgrims will eat almost anything at the end of the day. It was all washed down with a cheeky white wine. Ta dah! A young German girl called Miriam sampled the culinary delights too and even went back for seconds, then thirds. She then shared a glass of wine with her mate, Natasha. They skipped off into the night, whilst we settled into our bunks. Man City, my team, was playing Dave's "Spurs" this evening. He was quiet the next morning.

Cell Block "H"

Day Eight of the Camino. Navarette to Azorfa. (24.5k).

Well, let me tell you, Dave has certainly found his blinking legs. He sets off in the morning at a fair old rate. By the time I'm ready for a coffee, he's already there, coffee and tostadas in hand. I simply lag behind him and get to wherever we're going eventually.

Not much to report really today. It's Sunday and all is quiet. The weather has improved, spits and spots of rain early but the coat put away by 11am and I'm walking in a sodden, sweaty shirt. Breakfast at Ventosa and then on to Najera. Some of the outskirts in these small towns hide away the historic and fascinating centres.

On the way into Najera, a booted eagle soared above us for several minutes, picking up the thermals from the reddish-brown earth of the vineyards we wandered between. Snow-capped mountains have been on our righthand side for several hours. They are beautiful and imposing at the same time. Thankfully, we will not be venturing up any of their passes (Not yet at any rate!).

A long climb of maybe five kilometres out of Najera ensued. Over the tops to Azorfa. A bit of an unassuming place if I'm honest but a welcome sight nevertheless. After 20k+ each day, the legs are becoming weary and a bed and shower of any description are welcome. It's quite strange but as each day ends and the village of rest imperceptibly creeps towards us, how the Albergue of choice is always at the far end of it. Today is no different. We are staying in a municipal Albergue. As we rounded the street corner, it shocked our vision but not in a particularly good way. Dave commented that it looked like a prison block and he was right, but it's functional and only two per room. We have constantly encountered a guy called Nicholas from Denmark. A great bloke with a lovely disposition. Sadly, as we settle in the room adjacent to him, he has just informed us that he has to leave the Camino and return to Denmark. I have to say on his behalf that it was personal and unavoidable business that took him from the Camino. No illness or fatigue, certainly not, as he was always seemingly only a few hundred meters away from us on any stage of this "walk".

Wringing wet clothes, hung out of our ground floor window to dry, shower and fresh clothes on, we set off to explore our surroundings. No, sorry that's a small lie. As usual, we went to find a bar. Well, one has simply got to take on liquids at any given opportunity, don't you know?

Sat in a bar, sipping beer and watching the bedraggled pilgrims shuffle past. No matter what their age, at the end of the day, their pace and the gate is just the same. The two or three locals sat alongside barely give us a glance. Decades meeting the likes of us, entering their bar and using their hospitality must have become quite boring over the years. Today was clearly no different, although Dave and I did our best to keep the bell on the till ringing at a regular but gentle pace. One local had a small, black, scruffy dog. It had the run of the place. The owner held a lead, but I suspect it was never used. Each time the door of the bar opened, the dog would run out into the street, sniff the odd pilgrim, bark at no one in particular and then return under the table, duty done.

We have decided to cook another meal at "home" tonight. We had surveyed the kitchen and dining facilities at the Albergue. It wasn't hard to find. You entered the reception from a patio, which had a small cement pond/fountain, whose water was being blown asunder by the increasing wind. Once at the reception desk, you simply looked to the left and there it was. Long communal tables with benches. A partition wall with a triangular kitchen on the other side. Basic, very basic, but with everything we needed. Another culinary delight thrown together from my pasta range with a compulsory bottle of cheap wine. I don't know why, but I always seem to make enough for a small army.

This evening the army came in the shape of a 20-odd-year-old Dutch female, who I'd seen sat on a wall on the patio, cigarette between long spidery fingers.

She plonked herself across the table from us and engaged us in conversation. Usual stuff for pilgrims, 'Where are you from? Why are you doing the Camino? What's that you've cooked?'

She was almost salivating when her eyes asked, 'Any left for me?'

In fairness, she did look as if she needed a good hot meal inside her as she was fairly skinny, but there again, those of you who know Dave and I, you would say that most people look skinny in comparison.

Anyway, with her eyes doing the prompting, my mouth opened and the invite to help herself simply fell out. A big, broad smile lightened her face and she promptly produced a bottle of wine out of her large "hippy style" bag.

'Quits,' she said and went for a bowl.

Initially, I thought she was skinny because of the hunger suppression from smoking. No, she was simply bloody starving.

The first bowlful disappeared at a rate of knots, then a second, before, with a glint in her eye, she simply said, 'Can I?' She nodded to the pasta remains in the large bowl.

How could we refuse? 'Help yourself.'

And she did. Dave and I polished off the wine. Dave washed up and we left our Dutch girl, sorry but I can't recall her name, merrily chatting to a group of "younger" pilgrims. Time for "lights out".

Little milestones now. This is the completion of our first day of our second week. We have completed 220k!

No Horse Town

Camino Day Nine. From Azorfa to Redecilla Del Camino. (26.5k)

Good morning Camino blog readers. I hate to harp on about this but it's raining again and it's really cold. Ponchos on, we head out into the darkness at 07:20am. I have to say there's not much to write about when your view of the world is an area of pathway, two meters by one. Two hoods up (coat and poncho), and simply getting through it.

Today, we will mostly be talking about worms (again), tree pipits and storks, not forgetting a few massive vultures.

Before I become one of the Attenboroughs, I must just mention the thoughts that came into my head whilst walking behind Dave. We both look like the Hunchback of Notre Dame with our ponchos over our heads, as well as our rucksacks. Then it occurred to me that we should be called the two "caped crusaders", pilgrim reference here. And before any of the football team say it, "Fatman and Blobby". I'll leave it to Dave to pick which one he wants.

I digress, but my mind really does work in strange ways in these conditions. Much more than normal, anyway.

Back to the wildlife. The worms of Northern Spain are massive, more like small snakes. With my sight continually downwards, I see hundreds of them, and, as my GCSE Biology project was on worms, let me tell you that they come out in the rain for several reasons. It makes it easier for them to migrate to different areas. The rain vibrates the earth around them, which makes them think there are predators, ie moles, close by, so they surface to avoid them and finally some of the 4,400 species of worms surface in order to breed. The paths are running with water, it's a worm orgy if you can have such a thing as they are hermaphroditic. They have a "saddle", which contains both organs...sorry, I'm rambling again.

Around 9:30am, it was coffee break time in a tiny hamlet called Ciruenaat at the top of a very long climb. Post this, the wind came, cold and blustery but on the upside, the rain had stopped. Since Roncesvalles, Dave has repeatedly pointed out a bird at the top of a series of trees. It looks like a large sparrow from a distance. Anyway, this species of bird has appeared all along the route and only today did I get a close enough glimpse to establish that it was a tree pipit. Having never seen or heard one before, that's another ornithological box ticked.

We stopped for half an hour in Santo Domingo de la Calzada. Having put some energy in our legs, we set off and saw four huge vultures wheeling overhead. We trudged on to Granon and then our final destination, Redecilla de Camino. Upon leaving Santo Domingo, there were storks' nests everywhere to our right. On top of poles and two pairs of them on top of tall industrial chimneys. It was truly a lovely sight. Where both birds were in situ you could hear the clacking of beaks.

We booked into the municipal Albergue. I'm sure St James himself must have stayed here. No bar, no cafe, bugger all. Dave and I have been in some one-horse towns but this one, Redecilla Del Camino, hasn't even got a horse! Three of us are staying here tonight, everyone else has passed through. Not surprising. Highlight of the afternoon before we had our evening meal was the glass door of a display cabinet fell off its hinges. It didn't smash but Dave and I were entertained for 20 minutes, trying to put it back. I know you will find it hard to believe but the cabinet was being opened to get four small cans of beer out! We were paying for them, not robbing the cabinet! The pilgrim's menu that evening was a cosy candlelit dinner for Dave and I comprising of macaroni with tuna, microwaved chicken in a sauce with chips and bread, followed by a yoghurt. Basic but edible, and we were hungry. Oh, I nearly forgot, a small carafe of wine came with the meal. It went back into the kitchen, enough said about its bouquet and depth of flavour. Dave and I can drink almost anything but this was awful. We are not wine experts, but this must have been straight from the wine fountain back in Irache. We could have done with the candlelight bit too as it was freezing cold.

It's now 7:20pm and I'm tucked up already. The photo attached shows our dorm! Clothes drying and hung everywhere. The bunk beds haven't even got their own steps. The hostel has provided small step ladders, should any other pilgrim appear.

Dave and I are sharing this dreadful place with one other pilgrim, a French guy. He smiles a lot, and we try to converse a little in an Anglo French mix but his English is more limited than our French. So, it's Bonet de Duche from him and Petit Pois from me. You will see from the photograph that the sunlight is shining through the window. Don't let that fool you, its blinking freezing cold and it's another early night for the three of us.

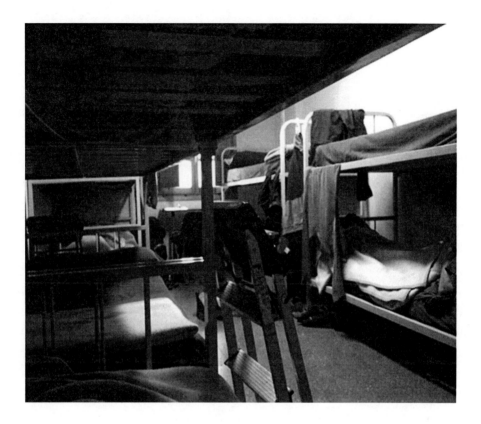

Luxury!

Keep the Noise Down, We're Australian!!

Camino Day Ten. Redecilla de Camino to Viilafranca Montes de Oca. 25k.

Continuing with the "horse" reference, we "bolted" from Redencilla around 07:30am. Clear blue sky but really chilly. The beautiful, rolling, green hills soon came under our feet and the toil and perspiration beset me. Dave commented that it reminded him of the "Downs", which apparently stretch from Kent to Portsmouth. I've never been but it must be lovely if it compares to this.

We reach Belorado by 10. A croissant and brew later we push on, but Dave again has gone off like an Exocet. He's like a man possessed. In truth, I become laboured and struggle to find any pace but "slow". Mid-morning, the sun sheds its shackles and the temperature climbs. It's really warm now but for some unknown reason I simply can't be bothered taking off my coat. Today I'm soaked inside! I've heard that when sailing ships are becalmed without wind or tide, they are said to be in the doldrums. Maybe my spirit and energy levels are in this limbo land.

We pass through lots of small hamlets, all have a church as their focal point. Most have pairs of storks nesting on them. There's Tosantos, Villambista and Espinosa before Villafranca Montes de Oca comes into view. In Villambista, I followed signs taking me off the Camino, which stated there was a cafe 200 meters to the right. Off I toddled, salivating at the thought of something hot and sweet. Ten minutes and several hundred yards later, I was furious. No cafe! Maybe it was out of season, but I could have done without the unnecessary diversion. Subsequently, I filled my water bottle from a four-spout fountain, which poured into its round deep base. I'm not sure where the water originated from, but it has floating piles of algae in it. I decide not to drink it. I press on, and as I leave Villambista, I can see Dave way off in the distance. He's only a few hundred yards from a village called Espinosa. He's easily one and a half kilometres ahead of me. As always, I can see him turn round, look back in my direction to ensure I'm following him, and he gives me a wave. In Espinosa, 2k further on, there's another fountain, which tinkles invitingly into a stone trough. A small sign alongside states that the water is only good for animals. The decision not to drink the water from Villambista earlier was a good decision on my part. That was until I'd realised I'd carried nearly a kilo of water for 3.5

kilometres for no purpose whatsoever! I could have kicked myself on the outskirts of Villafranca Montes de Oca as I poured it into the grass. You may not realise but every gram of extra weight you carry seems to multiply itself as the hours go by. Clearly, my "doldrums" have affected my ability to think logically.

The Albergue Dave had arrived at was fabulous. It is an Albergue attached to a lovely hotel. Any would-be pilgrim should consider this overnight oasis. I arrived at San Anton Ana's at 2:45pm. I was one weary traveller. Dave, God bless him, had booked us in and was sat waiting on the adjoining bed.

Shower, change and out of the dormitory part of the Albergue. We found the bar, which was closed until 4pm, so we walked a couple of hundred yards along the main road to a transport cafe/pub. The main road was thick with lorries and several were parked up on the open ground outside the pub.

Inside was welcoming and warm. Beer ordered and iPad plugged in to complete today's blog. Not much composing done in here though. We were engaged in conversation by a lovely Australian couple called Kim and Kevin. Both larger than life and travelling the Camino using whatever transport they could get their hands on. They had walked it two years earlier in the true pilgrim manner. Basic and not at all to the liking of Kim. But now, Kim was calling the tune. Apparently, their luggage was growing day by day, clothes, shoes and apparently anything she wanted. Kevin raised his eyes and sighed. It transpired that today she mainly wanted red wine. Nearly 4pm, so we drifted back to the hotel bar with the Aussies in tow. We didn't see our beds for a number of hours as we talked and drank our way from the bar to the restaurant and through a lovely pilgrim's meal in very luxurious surroundings. Quite a contrast between the two, really. Kim and Kevin were fabulous company, but does anyone have a volume control for her neck (she did apologise the next morning)? Post evening meal, we went to bed in the dorm, which comprised of around 12 beds. Not a good night's sleep. Lesley, the beautiful, young, French woman, whom we meet almost every day, suffered too. The snoring was awful and mainly came from the direction of two South Korean girls. They look so demure. You simply wouldn't believe it.

Kim took this photo of Dave and I whilst in the hotel bar. The smiles on our faces give away our tipsy state. Not drunk! Tipsy!

I have to say this…at the end of each day, it is difficult to function. To think straight or to get the right things out of our rucksacks or even remember where certain things are, and that's before we've had a drink. These days are testing in every sense. Buen Camino.

The Detective's Refuge, El Cid

Camino Day 11. From Villafranca Montes de Oca to Burgos. 38k.

Another bright and lovely day but a long toil up a steep ascent for a few kilometres that got the heart racing and the sweat running down our faces. Up into the pine forests but there were so many dead trees amongst the pines. Thousands of them all covered in a lichen of the palest green, almost silver. All it needed were "fairy lights" and it would have been like a gigantic grotto.

It was good to leave the constant thrum of the traffic as it careered along the N120. We have walked alongside this highway for quite some miles/days now. The forest, thankfully, seemed to go on for miles and probably did. Finally, we're out into the sun and gently undulating hills. Not quite as beautiful as yesterday's "Downs". Some lovely hamlets and villages, some I don't doubt with their own place in Spanish history, San Juan de Ortega, Ages and several more. The number of wind turbines is amazing. Row after row, they go on for miles and what's more they are all working! Unlike in the UK, where the vast majority seem to be frozen in time. The outskirts of the cathedral city of Burgos loom in front of us and directions for the airport can be seen at almost every junction. The "Camino Adventures" website, that I've become addicted to, advises all pilgrims to catch a bus from here. How right they were. Mile after mile of industrial units and then 8 storey apartment blocks. This went on for around nine kilometres. This is a bleak and depressing part of the Camino. It's not all beer and skittles!

However, the historic inner city is just beautiful. The tree lined avenues along the river, the stunning, historic architecture, the castle and the cathedral. WOW, the cathedral. I can honestly say that I have not, yet, seen a more incredible gothic monument to man's beliefs than this.

We found ourselves at a cafe just around the corner from the cathedral. We had promised ourselves a hotel room for the night on a further couple of occasions on the Camino, so whilst having a coffee, the iPad was switched on, password obtained, and the website "booking.com" entered.

Now last night, during the revelry with Kim and Kevin, they had mentioned that they too were staying in Burgos and had booked into a hotel called El CID. Apparently, their room looked straight out at the stunning cathedral less than 100 yards away.

Wouldn't you know it, the first hotel on the website was the same hotel. Not only that, but it was only 64 euros between Dave and me for the night. We didn't have to think twice. We booked it, closed the iPad, finished our coffee and set off to find the Hotel El CID. To our complete surprise, it was only 100 yards away around the corner. I think we arrived in the reception before my booking arrived on their computer. The receptionist double checked and having explained that we'd only booked it minutes ago, she found our reservation. Then, as we signed in and credit card details were taken, we heard familiar voices and an unmistakable woman's giggle. Kim and Kevin appeared. They were overjoyed with their room and said that maybe we would meet up somewhere later.

Off we went to our third-floor room, threw our rucksacks on our separate beds and stood back in amazement. Our window opened up above the cathedral square. We had uninterrupted views of this staggering architectural masterpiece. We simply gawped and then grinned like Cheshire cats. The next picture is the view from our room. I'd spend an awful lot more than the 64 euros it cost between us to stand all day just looking up in complete awe.

Now it's time for a treat. A deep, hot bath beckoned, and I needed my aching body soothing. Dave settled for a quick shower before I submerged myself and he set off for a "livener" before I met up with him.

The photograph above is the view from our room.

Another Grandad moment coming on. He would have loved this view, having been a master plasterer. We spent some time just people watching over a well earned coke. Then the tour of the cathedral with audio guide. It is an incredible building, some of it dates back to the early 13th century. Now here comes my Camino deliberation or call it what you will, maybe a rant or hissy fit. If somebody knows the answer to my next question, will they kindly tap me on the shoulder one day and make me understand?

Why does every facial expression, in religious pictures, statues, tapestry and every other aspect of the Christian religion get depicted without a smile? Not one inviting, welcoming expression can I ever recall, irrespective of the cathedral or church. All so bloody sombre and miserable. I thought religion was a celebration. This is just an observation, not an invitation for a punch up.

The above photo to enhance my previous observation!

We set about exploring the lovely narrow streets of Burgos. Liz from South Africa was coming out of a modern museum, which was unfortunately closing for the siesta. Maybe we would see her later. We felt the city come alive around 7:30pm. Throngs of people of every age cascading into the streets and filling the bars, cafes and restaurants. It was vibrant. We settled for pizza and another coke, yes coke! It was simply a regular evening in the city but if this is what it's like normally, I would love to visit when there's a celebration or fiesta.

We retired to our beds around 10pm after one more peak at that awesome cathedral.

When we were planning the Camino, Dave and I had promised ourselves that we would have two complete, separate days off during our walk. However, we found that we had toured where we wanted in Burgos and had enough relaxation and comfort so that we could continue walking first thing in the morning without losing a full day.

George the Giant and Lenin
from Belgium

Camino Day 12. From Burgos to Hornillos del Camino. 20.5k.

Before I start today's blog, yesterday was a milestone. Upon arriving in Burgos, we had completed 300k exactly.

Today was lovely. Just a top and shorts on and set off at 07:35am. The cool of the morning evaporated as we set a good pace through the suburbs of Burgos. Those precious few hours rest and a hot bath to soak away the aching muscles has put a spring in my step. I actually kept up with Dave. The terrain and views were unimpressive, for the most part. Swollen river, back alongside the N120 before we walked under a motorway and into the hills again. One thing both Dave and I noticed as we left the city of Burgos was the prison to our right. High walls and glass topped towers, just like a small airport control tower.

It seemed completely out of character with what we had seen in the old city but who knows who inhabits the eight storey apartments on the outskirts. I suppose I'm being a little out of order in my preconceptions here. I shouldn't have been surprised to see a prison, but I was. We arrived at Tardajos two hours and almost 10k later. Hot, sweet, black tea, which I've become accustomed to and a banana. Out through the rest of the small town, through a village called Rabe de las Calzadas and into a long but not too severe climb. A group of Vultures, 400 meters to our right, descended steeply. No doubt in my mind that they had found a carcass. However, it can't have been anything substantial as after a few minutes they were airborne again, riding the thermals which rose from the stony, brown fields.

We reached a crest and below us, maybe two and a half kilometres away was our destination, Hornillos Del Camino. Lots of pilgrims were strung out along the road before us and were descending upon this village. Fortunately, we had booked our beds in advance at an alberque called The Meeting Place. Yep, far end of the village again but what a fabulous oasis. So new, so clean. Immaculate showers, cooking facilities, a large, communal dining area and lawns with tables and chairs in which to relax and enjoy the warm sun. Laundry duties first. I take my socks, sweaty top and underwear into the shower with me. They won't take long to dry in the warmth of the sun this afternoon. This evening's communal meal, as advertised in the foyer, is a salad, bread, chicken and vegetable paella, lemon mousse with red wine and water; 9.50 euros. It's not worth cooking for yourself at this price.

Anyway, prior to that, we settled at a bar called Casa del Abuelo (literally translated to House of the Granddad), had a couple of beers and a ham and egg sandwich. The pilgrims already settled here were from every corner of the world. The mixture of languages, dialects and guttural tones were music to our ears. A "good to be alive" moment, as we took benefit of the warm sun. As we strolled into the patio area, we saw George. Remember him from Day Two or thereabouts? A mountain of a man, who was dragging all his possessions through the mud, stones and torrents of water in what looked like a granny's shopping trolley, with his dog, Lenin, a Belgian Shepherd, in tow. Smiles exchanged, confirmation of where we had last seen him, we got his update. He had been camping en route, rather than staying in Albergues, etc, out of choice, not just because he had a dog but because that's the way he wanted to complete the Camino. However, his tent had blown away and shredded itself on the branches of some trees one evening, in one of the storms we had encountered. He had spent the night in the pouring rain and a howling gale wrapped around his dog, trying to protect it whilst taking shelter under a tree. He said this lasted for about ten minutes before the dog, Lenin, became fed up and mooched about in the undergrowth, close to the tree trunk for a dry place. Following research, he has found at least 100 places to stay with his dog until Finisterre (maybe Elmo, my Catalan Sheepdog would enjoy the experience?). We talked to George for a short while. He is Italian and comes from Mirano in the north, next to the Austrian border. He trains police dogs. No wonder Lenin was so obedient.

Both Dave and I are very much in awe of him. He is one of those people you would just love to spend more time with and learn more about them and their lives. His dog is pretty special too.

View to Hornillos Del Camino from the crest. Dave extreme left of the three immediately in front. This photo typifies the walking of the Camino…when the sun shines.

Showered and onto the lawn. South African Liz had made it and we were joined by Fiona from Ireland and Chris from Hamburg. Sun beating down, washing drying, time to relax.

The evening meal was lovely. There were 19 of us at the "communal table". Liz from South Africa and Carmen from Namibia sat alongside. I have to say that it was the best paella I have ever eaten. Not just because we pilgrims will eat anything, nor because I was so hungry. It was simply the best. I even had seconds. The lemon yoghurt/mousse concoction for desert also had us smacking our lips.

Off to bed, still light, but we need our rest. Sadly, Dave and myself were short changed on the "rest" aspect, as it was another night of snoring from several of our fellow pilgrims, along with a constant door open, light invading the room, door closed, toilet flushed, door open…you get the picture.

Scrubbing Your Smalls

Camino Day 13. From Hornillos Del Camino to Castrojeriz. 21k.

First of all, a little "housekeeping". Can I apologise for any spelling mistakes in all of my blogs? Clearly, I am thankful for the corrections before they reach press. No excuses, i.e. 'I'm very tired or it was the blinking iPad, but I am tired!'

Secondly, this is the fabulous paella we ate last night. I forgot to add it to the last blog.

Day 13 started early, mainly due to the lack of sleep. Following a quick, strong, black, sweet coffee, we set off into the pre-dawn at 07:10am. It WAS chilly. Coats zipped up, off we trudged into the semi gloom. Another good pace from both of us, maybe I have finally found my legs? Who knows? But I am just grateful to be keeping up with Dave. After a climb for a number of kilometres, we level out. This is the "Meseta", the moors of Northern Spain. We knew that it was coming up and it goes on for the next few days. Piles of stones in tended, grass fields with little else but wind turbines.

Dave said to me, 'I spy with my little eye something beginning with WT.'

I replied, 'Weary Travellers!'

We were both right.

A sharp drop and the bell tower of the church in Hontanas appeared. Breakfast, a well earned tea/coffee and a banana. George and his dog, Lenin, were now part of the pilgrim caravan. We were with them for the rest of the day.

111

Almost imperceptibly, we walked downhill for most of the next 10k to Castrojeriz. We passed through the ruins of the San Anton Convent, which had been built in the 15th century. Not to miss a trick, an elderly gent had parked his dark blue car on the approach to the convent. Camino trinkets on display all around his car. He gestured to the pilgrims filtering past him. One or two paid a courteous inspection before moving on. Spanish guitar music drifted on the breeze as we ventured though the arches of the monastery that spanned the road. It was lovely and uplifting. If the Maestro has a collection tin in front of him, then I would contribute a few loose coins. It was so tranquil! We exited the shadows that the arches cast, only to find that the "flamenco guitar" was coming from an impromptu bar on the right of the road, just beyond the convent and sadly was not a live performance. How disappointing!

Castrojeriz now in sight

We ambled through the streets in the increasing heat. Our coats had been stuffed into our rucksacks some kilometres before. The Albergue Rosalia was difficult to find and the locals and street maps led us a merry dance for more than the so called ten minutes' walk. A nice Albergue, though, once we'd found it. So many different floors, all tiled and very uneven. Dormitories, front, left, right. Showers further right, kitchen, lounge on a large mezzanine floor and finally a quaint, first floor terrace. It was walled and with a stone sink, running cold water and a wooden wash board. What else could one do but spend a pleasant ten minutes scrubbing and rinsing our smalls.

Out and off to the shops to buy the evening meal. I'm cooking tonight. Pork chops, jacket potato, grilled tomato and mushrooms, bread served with a cheeky white wine, which is cooling as I write. Dave and I have struck an agreement. I cook and he washes the pots. The two supermarkets are just down the hill. Oh! Just a second, there's a small, welcoming bar to our left. It has a small patio, which captures the warm sun. Only one pint, though. You may get a small tapa, slice of tortilla with it, but at 3.50 euros per pint, one is enough, financially.

Prior to tea, the afternoon was spoilt a little by two younger men, maybe 20 or so. One German and one American. Three bottles of wine and two huge jars of sangria later, they appeared to be annoying everyone. Retrospectively, I believe that everyone deserves to let their hair down on the Camino at some point. As I write, I can only assume they have now fallen soundly asleep or have walked into town as the Albergue is quiet and sleepy.

We met Patty and Chris today in our little walled patio. Two pleasant Americans from Pennsylvania. Also, Tim from London. A sensible young lad who had jogged passed us earlier. He is going as far as Leon, before turning north to Oviedo, then Santander, Bilbao and finally San Sebastián. Oh, my lovely San Sebastián. Been there once, I'll never forget it. Beautiful, absolutely beautiful in so many ways. It captured my heart.

I have found myself a nice, quiet mezzanine hideaway within the multitude of floors and corridors. Electricity, Wi-Fi and peace. Blog time.

The evening meal was wholesome, and we even gave a pork chop and mushrooms to Tim, who had gone for the "ready meal" (Pot Noodle) earlier. It's now 7:40pm and I am already in my sleeping bag about to put my earplugs in. You may think that's ridiculously early but trust me, the rigours of the Camino truly find you out. A long, hard day awaits us tomorrow. I've worn earplugs every night and will do for the whole Camino. I dread to think what the nights would be like without them.

Tom, Dick and Harry

Camino, Day 14. Castrojeriz to Fromista. 26.5k.

I forgot to mention yesterday that whilst walking towards Castrojeriz a male hen harrier wafted across our path and simply glided over the green fields. It was as if it were a marionette held with the finest silk threads by a master puppeteer. It barely flapped and covered the ground from around 4' up just like an albatross skims the ocean waves. It was simply captivating.

And there was also Joanne. She is 40, looks 30 and was cooking an evening meal, along with Liz from South Africa, for a group of pilgrims. Joanne comes from the north island of New Zealand, where her parents run a farm. Last year, her friend wanted to visit Peru and so Joanne went along. Then onto Columbia, El Salvador, back to Columbia, Mexico, through the USA, into Canada and over to Europe, where after the Camino, she is going to Ireland. She has done this on her own as her friend returned home post Mexico. She has funded her passage by waitressing and various other jobs. What another remarkable human being. The world truly is a BIG place.

Today, Day 14, we set off at 06:55am. After 2k and in the gloom of early dawn, we were faced with a one in five climb for 1,050 meters. Alto de Mostelares was the name of the "hill". It was a good test. You can clearly see the path as it rises right to left as Dave hot foots it towards it.

The summit.

Dave on the Meseta. God, he loved the Meseta, NOT!

We crossed a stone bridge over the river Bisuerga. There's a pilgrim's hospital on the other side, where you can get your feet washed. However, before we reached the other side, we were accosted by swarms of midges and mosquitoes. We almost broke into a run. If my memory serves me correctly, this is where Heather Small on the recent BBC2 documentary, became offended and walked out of the hospital. I may be wrong, sorry if I am. Onto Itero de la Vega. A small village with a welcome cafe. "The usual please", tea and banana. Not much else to report re the walking front. Uninspiring views of fields, a brief stop in Boadilla, where I was literally robbed, 7 euros for a stale baguette with ham and cheese on and a coke!

The next 7k or so to our destination was boring. A rough pebble path along a canal, which brought us safely to Fromista. A town of no character. We had to double back on ourselves to find our Albergue for the night. If we had known what it was like, I'm sure that we wouldn't have booked it in advance. It's right on the side of a railway line, facing two large concrete buildings. As we crossed the raised, gravel car park towards the reception, our trepidation grew. We entered the reception, which was part of a large communal dining area in a dark, sombre, wood panelled room. Old, dusty wooden farm equipment adorned the walls. A man and a woman looked glumly at us. Took our money and stamped our passport with barely a word. The lady beckoned us outside and we followed her along a very long wooden veranda to the dormitory. The veranda ran parallel with the train track only yards away. Oh bollocks, this is so bleak and miserable. A hot bath and lovely Burgos were so far removed from this. I said to Dave that it's like the "camp" in the film, *The Great Escape*. We set about searching for Tom, Dick and Harry!

Our view from the entrance to our "camp".

Off into the town centre we went. A collection of bars around a crossroad. Tim, the jogger, going to San Sebastián, was ahead of us having arrived an hour earlier. He was chatting convivially to a young female. It would have been rude of us to interrupt. We just waved. We have spoken to one of the bar owners, who assures us he can get the Spurs versus Man United FA Cup semi-final on TV later this afternoon. So, there we were, sat in yet another bar with time to kill, hours in fact, before the match started. In the interim, our attention was drawn through the window and across the town square to where hundreds of pedal cyclists were being escorted by outriders on motorbikes. The whole of the little town seemed to be taking part in a miniature "Tour de Fromista".

If there were an ancient monument, church or anything of interest in this town, I'm sure we would have sought it out, but there wasn't. Tim joined us after a while. Tapas, beer, tapas, wine, ah, time for the football. Bless him, the landlord had promised us, but boy did he have a job finding the foreign channel. I think he would have been forced to try for hours, as we'd spent so much money in his bar.

Sadly for Dave, the game didn't go as he had hoped (and I had wanted). And it was an even more dreary walk back to "camp" and straight to bed. We had been joined by several other inmates by this time, two American ladies and several South Koreans, who were huddled up in their bunks as we returned. Heck was it cold. Layers of "horse blankets" over us as we curled up in our sleeping bags. I don't know what time it was but the late night train thundered through in the dark. It was like an old black and white comedy film, where everything rattles and shakes. It must have been going at quite a lick. When I say 'late night train,' it may only have been 9:30pm for all I knew.

Eight Twelves Are?

Camino. Day 15. From Fromista to Carrion de Los Condes. 21k.

Up early. Disturbed night in the camp. Tim was already up and returning from the showers. He confirmed that they were hot and clean. Just what we needed, some warmth in our bodies before we set off. In and down we went until at 07:10am, Dave popped out of "Tom" whilst I popped out of "Harry" (well, you didn't expect me to use the third tunnel name just for a smutty little piece of journalism, did you?).

Cool and with a cloud covering, we set off through Fromista again. Pilgrims already in front and behind. The first three kilometres took us to Poblacion de Campos. A sleepy little village but with a cafe that was open. I'm becoming addicted to tea without milk. Off again a few minutes later. Not much to report today as the panorama is boring to say the least. Grey paths, regimented rows or copses of poplar trees. The path split. Follow the road or head into the fields? The fields just edged it. More of the same, sadly, only the path took us down the side of the river Ucieza. Warblers calling (I nearly said warbling!) all along the banks. As boredom beset us, I invented a time-consuming game of "rutting" (I bet that's got your smutty interest!). Anyway, the paths are stony and set hard with mud. They are extremely rutted from tractors, pilgrims and other Godly creatures. The game is to pick the rut to walk along that is less severe on the feet and knees. Constantly changing every 20 or so yards, it seemed to go on for ages meandering from rut to rut. Other villages came and went. Nothing open, no respite. Via Villamentero de Campos we rejoined the road. A never-ending straight line of gravel, full of pilgrims. So glad we keep booking our Albergues in advance. On through Villalazar de Sirga, where we had another short break, although we had to leave the Camino to find a cafe that was open, and on towards our destination Carrion De Los Condes and the Monistario de Santa Clara, where our beds await. I'm really sorry at this point but there really isn't much to convey to anyone who reads this. The truth of the matter is that it's that boring that Dave confessed to doing the 12 times table in his head and then we tried to recall all the FA Cup winning teams since 1966, in order.

The town arrived at our feet and the monastery was only a couple of hundred yards into the town. Ah, there's a change! It was lovely. A complete contrast to yesterday. Quiet, calm, peaceful and yes, holy.

126

We were greeted by an enthusiastic man called Ignacio in the reception come trinket shop. A young married couple with their daughter were booking a tour of the monastery. Ignacio explained everything, escorted us to our three bedded, simple, clean and very humble quarters. Tim, the jogger, was lodging with us tonight.

Washing machine and dryer sorted, shower, make our beds and into the town for lunch. Before I continue, I must point out that quite often now, as we book into the Albergues we are handed paper mattress covers and paper pillowcases. They are hygienic, disposable and a necessity, as who knows who has slept in the bunk beds before. We settled in Bar Espana. So much better than yesterday. It's lifted our spirits somewhat, but we are aware that tomorrow will be a difficult day. Long, 26k, flat Maseta, no resting place for the first 17k. The rest this afternoon will do us good.

Into the town. Boy, do these Spaniards know how to charge pilgrims, we are pilgrims for heaven's sake, not just off our yacht in Marbella. The beer in Bar Espana was 3.50 euro per pint. On the upside, it did offer a variety. There were golden, dark and stout coloured beers. We tried a couple but not all three and we drank small beers! Off in search of a cheaper place, where we were joined by Tim and two American ladies, Barbara and Jackie. Late afternoon, a meal of pizza, Caesar salad and a bottle of white wine was ordered. Our companions were all good company, and we got the ladies to model our sponsored T-shirts and then sign them. This continued the evening tradition as the days went by.

Bed just after 8pm. Boy, it's cold in the monastery.

Dave and "Tim the Legs".
He's ran every day, at least a half marathon. He's a great guy.

Barbara, Tim and Jackie. Well, it's better than keep seeing us in the sponsors' T-shirts.

Hugs and Tears

Camino. Day 16. Carrion de las Condes to Teradillos de Los Templarios. 27K.

Well my little couch pilgrims, (only joking), what a start to a difficult day. David mistakenly got up at 5:40am. I waited in the dark for another half hour, trying to rearrange my bedding to eke out the last of the warmth. I succumbed and rose, collected my towel and toiletries. Off I slumped into the dark corridor. One of the two toilet/showers was occupied but the light shining under the door was suddenly extinguished by the occupant. A shadow in the gloom approached and it wasn't until that we were two feet apart that we looked at each other. The waxen, round, white face of Iris looked at me and then me back at her. It took a split second and then the recognition exploded in beaming smiles. She threw her arms around my neck, squealed, hugged me to pieces and jumped up and down. Unfortunately, she was now wearing hiking boots and I only had flip flops on. Who cares? I hugged her too. I tried to explain that I couldn't believe that she had made it all this way. Her luggage had clearly arrived but the drive in this young woman must be burning bright and so intense. We parted, beaming smiles and she disappeared into the pre-dawn gloom like an ethereal spirit.

I walked into the bathroom, turned on the light and stared into the mirror, shaking my head in disbelief. I have to confess to having a lump in my throat and moist eyes as I write this section. Some things that happen on the Camino simply blow your emotional socks off.

We passed each other several times this day. She had linked up with a Chinese-American girl and a Chinese lad called Nathan, both of whom translated for her. Her English was better than my Mandarin but sometimes you don't need words.

We had coffee in the kitchen where Tim joined us. It was time for him to depart and head to Oviedo. He donated his energy bars to us as he would no longer need them and I promised to keep him up to date with the blog and gave him the details of where to find us in Portobello Bar, Campoverde.

Dave and I set off as the bell in the Monastery chimed 07:00am. Unfortunately, we couldn't stay behind until 09:30am in order to hear the monks sing. Out into the chilly morning and out of the town. Long, long, long flat path out into the country winding its way into the fields.

The first Camino casualty. A lovely, vibrant green gecko, who had recently lost the end of its tail. I do hope that it wasn't via a pilgrim's boot.

Dave put his music on via his earphones and I listened to the bird song. Cuckoos, blackbirds, pipits, chaffinches, great tits, blue tits, an eagle owl in the distance with its cackle drifting for several kilometres and yes, warblers warbling! Music to my ears, at any rate. Ten kilometres under our feet and a seasonal cafe opened on the right. BBQ already lit and sausages on the go, we settled for tea, coffee and one of Tim's energy bars. This first stop was very welcome. It had been another long morning. Dave made friends with a lovely Boxer dog and explained how he once owned one with the same markings. My mind wandered to Cleo, our Boxer. She was beautiful, if you can use that term for a Boxer. She wasn't of brindle markings but red with white socks and chest. She only had three legs too, but that's a story for another day.

Another 7k until Calzadill de la Cueza. Head down, bottom up. I put my music on, Andrea Bocelli. I don't know why but as soon as he started singing, it opened up the flood gates. Emotions just swamped me. I was so glad that Dave was behind and couldn't see, but I know he would have pulled me together. Dave had conveniently nipped off for an impromptu pee behind a barn wall. What he hadn't seen was the coach load of Japanese tourists with their Nikon's extended in his direction.

Two hours later we had another stop, around 11am. Lesley, the French girl, was already there and other pilgrims were pouring over the horizon 500 meters back. These included four South Koreans, two lads and two girls, all in their mid-twenties.

Dave and I ate Spanish sausage and a form of salad with an assortment of beans/peas. It was all washed down with a coke. Not the South Koreans! Their table was covered in an assortment of food. Salad, bread, a plate full of sausages, eggs and there before our very eyes, four large tankards of beer. We watched in amazement as it was all devoured amongst a constant, undecipherable chatter. Even Dave and I don't succumb to beer this early.

Off we set again, fully refreshed, but the next few hours became tormented. For some reason, the nearer our goal became, as shown on Dave's GPS, the longer it took us to get there. When we finally saw the village of Terradillos de Los Templarios, it seemed like a mirage. The sun was getting to me. I knew that our final destination of the day was off the main road and via narrow side streets that all descend to its gates. We arrived at the lovely Albergue, Jacques de Molay, early in the afternoon.

A room of our own, only ten euros each. Communal but clean showers and toilets and a lovely garden. It also had a fabulous, typical old Spanish dining area.

The early afternoon took its course and we settled in the garden. A group of a dozen Pilgrims, all wearing the same green T-shirts on with a logo, took over a small terrace. They were excited, giddy and probably a little tipsy as the beer flowed amongst them. Every few seconds, their conversation would have them erupting with laughter. It brought a spirit of "Bon ami" to the lush, warm gardens. Then they were gone, and tranquillity descended. That was until Iris and her interpreters arrived. Over they came and she presented Dave and me with a gift, each wrapped in brown paper. There before us were two beautifully hand painted tiles/fridge magnets. She explained that it was just a small "Thank You" for getting her through that torrid first day and giving her the strength to carry on. Oh, what a lovely woman. Well, we thought that she was a young girl, she certainly belied the fact that she was a mature woman with teenage children.

Two more pilgrims, Thomas and Christian, joined the throng. These German guys had been on the Camino for a few days now. Thomas is a priest and each year, he takes a week off, joins Christian, and together they have walked the Camino section by section, only their Camino started in Germany many years ago and it transpires that they had walked over 2000 kilometres to this point. This year, they are going as far as Leon, maybe two days ahead.

The evening meal was ten euros too. Well, it makes things easy for the taxman. The meal itself was good, wholesome and filling. Rabbit with a sauce and rice, chicken and chips and Arroz con Leche, plus wine and water.

We were joined at the table by a quiet Canadian guy called Gilles. He portrayed a sad and lonely figure and told us that he was on the Camino because his marriage had broken up. It had been his wife's decision, and it had clearly come as a severe blow. Although this was not a recent event, he clearly could not come to terms with it. We didn't pry, it didn't seem appropriate.

It had been a hard day, but the resting place made it all worthwhile.

Footnote by Debbie Coupe's research…

Dave informs me that Jacques de Malay was the 23rd grandmaster and final knight to join the Knights Templar. In March 1314, he and a few other templars, after enduring torture and many other humiliations, were sentenced to death. He knew that this was as a result of plots and whilst dying, he cursed everyone who had recommended his execution. What a coincidence on St George's Day. I'll raise another glass to that!

From Eartha Kitt to the Hobbits in 4k

Camino Day 17. From Terradillos de Los Templarios to Bercianos Del Real Camino. 24.85k.

It's 07:10am and a cool breeze meets us as we step beyond the garden walls of our Albergue. It's a clear sky and indication of a hot day ahead. It didn't disappoint. We had barely walked one kilometre and had just edged into the rolling countryside, when a female pilgrim sidled up alongside me. Dave, as ever, was a few meters ahead. She was in her 60s, tanned and had a weather-beaten face. Pilgrim staff in her right hand and the latest iPhone in her left. She begged me to listen to the music that she was about to play. Her iPhone screen read "Songs of the Camino". The music was really quite sombre but in this cool light, it was if the monks from the previous day had joined us. It was all in Spanish, but I understood that the lyrics were all about getting to the end, not just of the Camino, but life itself. To be strong and courageous. And then my little female pilgrim burst into song; it must have been the chorus. She had a deep gravelly voice which matched her smoky, tobacco-wrinkled complexion. If I had closed my eyes, I'm sure I would have been listening to Eartha Kitt. It came to an end and I told her that I had enjoyed it, I had. It was a lovely thing for her to do. Onwards and through the flowing countryside with the sun now at our backs and it's starting to warm the day. We had travelled only another three kilometres when we rounded a bend and there it was before us. I could have sworn it was Bilbo Baggins' house out of the Hobbit. Not just one door into the hillside but several. Chimneys poking up above the mounds topped with grass, a house with a domed roof or should I say hillock.

Our very own Hobbit

It wasn't called "The Wold", just Moratinos. A quick, five-minute stop at a cafe across the road, which unfortunately was not operated by Hobbits.

On through San Nicholas Del Real Camino (I'm not sure why this part of the Camino is "Royal", I will have to research when I get time). This town should have had a flock of llamas with a group of Peruvians playing the panpipes in front of the church. All the trees had bunting on them and on their trunks, they wore knitted blankets made up of numerous squares, just like the ones my nana made. Quite a strange sight and it was way too early to find anyone to ask of their significance.

The day and the paths stretched out before us towards Sahagun and I have to confess to some considerable fatigue at this point. I watched Dave turn 90 degrees to the right, away from the main road. I was bemused as I could see the city of Sahagun looming up in front of me some two kilometres straight ahead. However, this detour was worth it, as it led to the beautiful old chapel of Ermita Virgin Del Puente. This tiny chapel was built in the 12th century and was also a hospital for troubled pilgrims.

The pathway away from the "Ermita" was then further adorned by two statues in its grounds, which guarded the way forwards. These statues are of Bernardo de Sedriac, died 1128, who founded the local Cluniac Abbey and King Alfonso VI, "The Brave", 1047-1109, who founded the city of Sahagun.

Sahagun is a large, uninspiring, industrial town with a railway station. We crossed into the centre and had a tea/coffee break. It was very welcome. The final energy bar from Tim and we were off again. As we exited Sahagun, I managed to capture what I assumed was the only interesting view of the city, prior to leaving

Nothing much to report on this final 10k of the day. It was hard going, boring and getting very warm. We stopped for a coke in Calzada Del Coto. It was a 300-meter diversion over the A231, but it was needed. Into Bercianos Del Real Camino and to our rustic Albergue. Through an uninviting door sized hole in a wall, a terrace with tables and chairs, a few plants, trees and a bar/reception appeared ahead. It was a small oasis. Nine euros each for a bunk bed. We share a room with two others and have a small adjoining room with four bunks occupied by a French couple and their two young children. Rustic, that fits us perfectly.

All showered, clothing washed and sorted; its blog time. But not before Dave finds a space on the wall-mounted clothesline. Spooky, he found the precise gap between a bra and a pair of red knickers. Well, I say knickers when I mean thong. Well, I say thong when I actually mean catapult! Really, where's the female who needs medical attention for chafing?

Partway through my deliberations, I crossed the terrace to the bar for a couple of small beers. There's a lady sat on her own at a table with a bowl full of something. Being nosey, well, it was part of my job once upon a time, I peered over. I recognised the contents instantly. They were Percebes, or more commonly known as The Goose Foot Barnacles. They are a very expensive delicacy. They grow on the rocks, which are lashed by the sea in Galicia. Several people per year are killed trying to prize them from the rocks whilst constantly trying to evade the huge waves of that coastline. Thankfully, the lady offered me one. I explained in my poor Spanish that I knew what they were and that they were expensive. She agreed but told me it was a gift. They taste like most any other whelk or mussel, etc. The thought of people dying for these small creatures added to the gastronomic experience but only in a poignant way. Strangely enough, post beer purchase, our host and landlord brought out the typical pieces of tortilla but this time they were accompanied by a small dish containing seven or eight Percebes. A lovely and generous gesture.

******

Camino fact…the Percebe is nothing more than a shell with a large penis inside. It has the largest penis pro rata with its body than any other creature on earth! Now there's something you never thought you'd read in my blog! I'd just like to thank Alex Polizzi for that fact, who recounted it during one of her programmes whilst exploring the whole of Spain. Dave did crack a funny at this time but it's not going in this Booker Prize winning piece of literature. Well, it was something including the words, "only, time, penis, my and mouth".

Dave has now got the precise GPS kilometres that we have walked…stand by for the total…drumroll please…441.59k.

According to the T-shirts worn by the bar staff where we are, there are only 357k more to do until we reach Santiago de Compostela. Two weeks today, hopefully.

We have just finished tea. We planned to cook at the Albergue but the local mini market wasn't up to much, so we returned to the funky bar, where we'd had a quick drink in earlier. We both ordered a hamburger and chips. Not Michelin star but one hell of a burger. Two pâtés, German smoked ham, bacon, cheese, lettuce, tomato, fried onion and an egg. An absolute feast to two hungry pilgrims. Back to the Albergue, one nightcap with a Mars Bar and off to bed shortly to rest our aching limbs. We tip-toe around the small dormitory so we don't disturb the French children next door.

One Coffee, One Banana and One Tea Equals 20k

Camino. Day 18. From Bercianos Del Real Camino to Mansilla de Mulas. 27.5k.

What can I say about this leg of the Camino? Well, we were up early, after deciding not to watch the football last night. Following one of the better coffees served by our host, we were off into the pre-dawn light at 06:50am. A lovely morning with the promise of much sun again. The cool breeze lifted our spirits as we set about the hard slog that was ahead. We hadn't got a clue! It was 7k to the first stop and tea/banana, El Burgo Ranero. Most of our companions stopped here. It had been 7k of nothing. No scenery, a pressed, uneven gravel path alongside a road. If you wanted another picture of a stork nesting on a church, I could have taken a photo. As it happened, I couldn't be bothered. We pressed on, refreshed. The sun was up in the clear blue sky and it was warming up nicely. But at this point, I have nothing whatsoever to write. It was mind numbingly tortuous. A constant path alongside a never-ending road. Flat, boring and crippling to every sense and muscle. I'm sure that if there was something to distract the mind, it would have been more enjoyable. 13 kilometres along this road, although you may as well add a nought to that for all it mattered, we stopped for lunch at 11:40am, Reliegos. Beef baguette and a coke. It was a strange bar/restaurant, but it was the first one and a welcome sight. It played rock music. The girl behind the bar had dyed pink and purple hair and a tie-dyed shirt on. She seemed to like her music. Eartha Kitt (Old Tobacco Face) was there too, it was definitely her scene.

The journey to the bar had been that stupefying that Dave took a photo of some cows and their calves in a field.

We knew that we only had 6k more to go and set off at a plod. Feet so tired that they were hardly lifted and scuffed the gravel below. It was hot and getting hotter. Forecast 26 degrees. Better get a move on. If only we could. We could see our destination in the heat haze, but it simply would not come nearer. To make things worse, as we finally stumbled into town, every joint and muscle aching and sweat pouring out of every pore, we were greeted by a sign on the right of the roadside, "Albergue Jardin Del Camino 150 meters". What a load of tosh, it was at least 500 meters away, but it had done the job of keeping us going. It's a lovely place.

We turned right off the road and into the grounds laid to lawn. Fellow pilgrims were already seated at tables with tapas and beer. At first, we saw the Kiwi, Joanne. She said 'Hi' and used our names. A figure in black, back towards us, heard her speak. He turned and stood up instantly. Ritchie, who else? His long black hair, lean frame and glasses. Some expletives and hugs were exchanged. Apparently, he hadn't made his mind up where to stay tonight and was thinking of going on to Leon. He booked in shortly after us. This blinking Camino does it almost every day. From the depths of pain and suffering comes a shining beacon of light. Now, at the time of writing most of this blog, we are sat with Ritchie, Joanne, Thomas, a German priest, and Christian, his friend, were there too, this being their penultimate day. Tomorrow, they leave Leon for Madrid and a flight home. Their 2018 week complete.

There are two American guys joining the party. One is called Clyde and his brother-in-law Mark. Clyde lives in the Rocky Mountains. He thought he'd trained for this, he hadn't! He has just called it a 500-mile pub crawl! Then he looked down at his feet and changed his mind.

An Australian couple, Gary and Eileen, joined the merry throng. I mention them chiefly because of "his" views on Brexit. We had a heated debate. Then the topic of the Camino resurfaced. In a small contrast to the comment above by Clyde, Gary called it an "800k long psychiatric couch"! Nothing to choose between them, both quite accurate.

It's 8:45pms. Another pizza for tea and off to bed in a split dormitory of 48 pilgrims. Well, what do you expect for five euros?

Michael Jackson Live in Leon

Camino. Day 19. Mancilla de Mulas to Leon. 24k.

The number of pilgrims is growing. So many are on the paths before us and we think we are setting off early! It's 6:55am again. Out of town and yet more roadside paths with nothing to report. It's a four-and-a-half-hour slog into Leon. The suburbs are much the same as Burgos. Industrial with tenements from the 60s/70s. It all seems so tired and uninteresting. The city centre, however, is vibrant. Not as pretty as Burgos but it has a nice cathedral, plaza mayor and enough side streets to keep you occupied. However, it's off to our hotel first, the 4* Conde Luna. It must have been 4* some years ago, as it too is tired, but it has comfy beds and hot showers that work properly and toilet roll. Finally, booked in, we set off to explore the city. Off to where else but the main square, where we see some familiar faces.

The bar we settle at is called El Reloj (the clock) and it's right in front of the cathedral. We have found that a coffee and a "tapa", comprising of a petite sandwich, is only 1.50 euros, Happy days. Gilles from Canada joins us, along with Miriam from Holland. It transpires that Miriam and two of her friends have donated to our Givey website, thanks ladies. Thomas and Christian arrive; it's their last full day.

Gilles has clearly forgotten that he had told us the tale of his separation before. I nodded, told him I understood his pain and gave him support at the right places once again. There's something missing in his tale. I can't quite put my finger on it. Not yet, at any rate. It comes to Dave and me in the coming hours and the subject resurrects itself some days later.

Inside the bar, "Radio Castillo Y Leon" are setting up to broadcast. Maybe they'll interview us and spread the Dave and Steve Camino story. Not a bit of it. A team of at least eight pretentious so and sos, one with a dickie bow and another one who is simply full of himself, are doing a live "wine tasting" on radio. What a sodding nerve! Five bottles of free wine in front of them and at least five complementary dishes of food to accompany it. I sit alone inside the cafe/bar, waiting for my iPad to charge and watch the sickening pantomime unfold. As I'm sat there, fuming at the sickening audacity of it all. My sight wanders out through the window and to events in the cathedral square.

Not 20 yards away are a male and female beggar. They are pestering the pilgrims and passers-by. I say 'pestering' because she is pleading with the pilgrims for money. She tells them how destitute she is and that her children have nothing. Then, without warning, her mobile phone rings. Unashamedly, she just turns her back on her victim, delves deep into her rags and pulls out a mobile phone. She shares a joke with a friend on the other end and then back to business with another victim.

I really don't know which of the two scenes offends me most.

Dave and I decide to "accost" two elderly ladies behind us. We ask them if they would like to put on our sponsored T-shirts. They agree and tell us that they are from the Netherlands, not Holland, and we ask them to sign our shirts.

Nelly and Ricky were their names, but we realise that we have missed a trick here. We should have got all our fellow pilgrims, the special ones, to sign the shirts too. We set about rectifying this, hopefully not too late. I decided to retire to the hotel at this point for a siesta. Dave continues touring the city. A couple of hours later, I call him. I can hear music in the background. He gleefully informs me, 'I'm watching Michael Jackson.'

So, he must be, as I can hear the lyrics and beat of "Billy Jean" booming away in the background. I tell him that I will find him if he stays put.

Sure enough, it doesn't take long. A woman has set a cloth on the ground. There's a box on the cloth, acting as a stage and she controls a foot-high marionette of Michael Jackson. He's dressed in a black suit, black hat and white shirt and gloves. A crowd of thirty or so tourists are captivated as she moves the figure precisely to the beat as it imitates the star himself perfectly. It really was entertaining and put smiles on everyone's faces. I'm just sad that I can't attach Dave's video to my blog. I'm sure you would have enjoyed it.

Off we went, meandering around the narrow, bustling streets trying to find cheaper meals. We did but they weren't good.

It's gone 8pm and I'm typing this blog sat on my bed and Dave is reading across the room. Our bodies will needlessly wake us at 6am and I suspect we will be beyond Leon city limits not too long after that.

Below are some of the more interesting parts of Leon.

I've only included this picture as Dave is a big Spurs fan. I think it says it all.

Every Day is Christmas on the Camino

Camino. Day 20. Leon to Villar de Mazariffe. 22k.

It was a cold start to the day at 7am. Even the warmth of the hotel couldn't keep us shackled for long.

Leon has mountains completely wrapped around it. They are still snow capped, with more snow to come in the next couple of days. The photo below shows just how flat the Meseta is before the climbs begin again.

The morning breeze had a bite to it. It sharpened our senses as we walked up through the suburbs. We saw Thomas and Christian make their way into the bus station, which is situated between the river and football stadium. They were on their way back to Germany. Buen Camino mis amigos hasta ano proximo…

We thought the trip into Leon was bleak but leaving Leon was worse for around 8k. There were industrial estates, recycling plants, rubbish dumps and more industry. Simply awful.

The Camino followed the main road out of the city until we reached La Virgen Del Camino. Time for hot refreshment at a small, corner cafe, at the side of the busy road and then we swerved off to the left and blissfully away from traffic and civilisation. Gentle rolling countryside with tiny hamlets stretched for many kilometres. A small incline and out onto the open moors. I kicked on and for once left Dave. I felt alive today. I'm not sure where it came from, but I hope this feeling continues until the end. On the birdwatching front, there was another black kite majestically riding the breeze and an eagle to our right but just a little too far away to correctly determine the species.

Another 7k to Oncina de la Valdoncina. The breeze had turned into a constant burning, cold wind, sweeping down off the black, intimidating, silhouetted mountains. The peaks of almost every one of them was covered in snow. Dave and I both knew that in the next few days there are two long and intense climbs out there in the distance. The one in a week's time was the most foreboding.

Oncina de la Valdoncina was an unremarkable village, apart from one thing, not one person was on the street. It was a ghost town. We had to walk to the far end of it to find an open, welcoming, bar, but not a blinking soul. They clearly knew it was a day for toasting your toes in front of an open fire. Following the lines of pilgrims traipsing into Leon, it was strange to see just four of them in and around this village.

As we left the bar, the wind intensified to such a degree that it forced us to put our hoods up. It was blinking cold.

The sun, though, had teased the slumbering foliage out on every tree and bush in recent days but this was a false dawn before spring would arrive in earnest weeks later. Rain and snow are set to hinder our progress over the next couple of days, according to the weather forecast.

The final stretch of road to today's destination, Villar de Mazariffe, was flat for five kilometres and ran through rapeseed fields, all yellow and dancing in the wind, (no, I'm not Wordsworth!). Around one kilometre before Villa de Mazariffe, dozens of teenage lads cycled past us, going in the opposite direction. They were fresh faced and wore T-shirts and shorts. They were accompanied by a number of older men whom I assume were their teachers. Did they know something which lay ahead? I hope not.

At the start of the village was a small pond and a pilgrim resting area on the right invited us to stop but the bitter cold forced us to find the warmth of our Albergue. The Tio Pepe Albergue (sherry, now there's a thought) was situated, once again, in front of the little chapel adorned by storks and their massive nests. The view from my bunk also had the foreboding mountains of future days.

The Albergue is fine but the menu is a little restricted and they don't have a kitchen so that we could cook for ourselves.

There are large bottles of cider on offer at three euros, just right for parched pilgrims. We split the bottle. Homemade, with just the right amount of sediment in the bottom! Hell's teeth, it was rough.

An American couple called Ning and John were sat at an adjoining table in the courtyard area. The usual conversation started, and they informed us that they were from New Orleans. They asked me to take a photo of them and I obliged. The next thing I knew was that Ning had produced two "pin broaches" for Dave and myself. They had apparently been blessed by their local priest, a lovely gesture.

As we sit here writing our blogs, we realise that we have now covered 508k, give or take a few meters. We are now spending more and more time planning ahead and may be stretching ourselves a little too far in our daily walking aspirations. We are already booked into an Albergue in Astoria tomorrow but have told them we may not arrive until 4pm as it will be a long and slow 30k+ day.

Just for a few minutes, I drift off, my attention drawn by distant movement. From my seated position in the bar (we've moved out of the cold courtyard), I can see through the window up to the chapel tower, where there are three storks' nests.

One left, one right, one penthouse. A pair of mature birds to each. Clearly one stork sitting on their precious eggs whilst the other attentively stands guard. All of a sudden, the guard on the right-hand nest commences to do its mating dance. Wings spread wide and then thrown back whilst its long neck is stretched head to the sky. In an instant, the head is jerked backwards and it's neck and head lie upside down along the full length of its back. This was repeated just enough times to coax its partner off the eggs. They "clack" beaks together and she settles again. Just bonding.

In the midst of my reverie, I also notice that several cheeky sparrows are flitting in and out of their "sublet apartments" within the metre-deep piles of carefully placed sticks which lie beneath the storks.

I've also just noticed the red, slightly out of season, Christmas reindeer on the windowsill. It's Christmas every day on the Camino.

The afternoon drew to a lazy close and we walked a few steps to a more modern bar with Wi-Fi and chicken and chips. We dined with a fabulous 71-year-old American lady called Rita from Huston. She was ex-military. We discussed the gun law in the US, well, it was an open door for us. In return, she was so interested in our Camino cause, i.e. the orphanage and AECC. It turns out her that husband is suffering from cancer and it's one of the reasons she is on the Camino by herself.

It's nearly 8pm. We are sharing our room with a father and son from South Korea.

Sweet dreams.

1975 Revisited

Camino. Day 21. Villarreal de Mazariffe to Astorga. 32k.

Before I commence today's recollection, something has occurred to me. This is the end of our third week walking, plus those days travelling to the start of the Camino, and on each and every day's, blog I have mentioned "drinking" by both Dave and I. I have to say that it's true BUT we have never over indulged, become drunk or had a hangover. We have drank responsibly for two chief reasons, a) we simply would not be able to complete the Camino being continually hungover, b) and just as equally important, we thoroughly enjoyed the "Bon Ami" of our fellow pilgrims. Their tales, experiences and life stories were the real drug of choice. Oh, one more reason, funds.

It had been excessively warm in our cosy, four-bed room last night. So much so that I was awake early but didn't go to wash until 6am. Creeping about, trying not to wake your roommates at that time in the morning is really difficult.

In any event, Dave and I were downstairs by 06:35am and waiting for somebody to arrive to open up the bar area for breakfast, at least a coffee. Nothing, so at 06:50am we were off. Still cool and barely any light to guide us due to low grey cloud. From the outskirts of the slumbering village, there it was laid out before us. The longest, straightest road I can recall. Absolutely arrow straight, flat and running for 6k. Head down and bottom up again. Even though we had set off early, unbelievably, there were still one or two pilgrims ahead of us.

Half a kilometre from the end of this stretch, we could see a village to the left and another to the right. Both only 300 or 400 meters either side. I asked Dave which one our path would turn to.

He replied, 'What if it goes straight on?'

Wouldn't you blinking well know it, it did. Onto a dusty path with pebbles and the start of an Olympic version of "rutting". After a few kilometres, we found ourselves in a village called Villavante. In a lovely clean Albergue in the middle of nowhere, we had a quick hot drink before we pressed on and an hour later, we entered Hospital de Orbigo. Apparently, it is of historic importance due to its bridge and the field to the left of it, where they still joust.

Just time for one more cup of tea before we press on to Astorga.

Leaving Hospital de Orbigo, we had two options, the country route or the one alongside the N120 again. Sorry to disappoint but we took the latter, as it allegedly was one hour and 15 minutes shorter. You could have fooled me! Time for some music courtesy of DJ Don Stu. I chose Elbow, the "Seldom Seen Kid" album, followed by Supertramp's "Crime of the Century" album from 1975. Considering its over 40 years old, it was just great to hear it again. I remembered every word and it took me back to 1977, when I saw them live at the Palace Theatre in Manchester. They had just brought out "Crisis, What Crisis" at that point. Happy memories that occupied my mind with the kilometres disappearing under my feet.

Finally, after what seemed like an eternity, Astorga was in view but so too were the snow-capped, black mountains from yesterday that now loomed menacingly in front of us.

Below is a crucifix just before the descent towards Astorga. Then there was a water fountain depicting an ancient pilgrim at the base of the hill. This was tended by an elderly local guy, who was filling up water canisters. He had been at the crucifix earlier but had arrived before us by car. He was engaging virtually every pilgrim who passed him in conversation.

Into the suburbs of Astorga and a glass of coke before the final 4k of the day.

As I may have mentioned, Dave had told me that it was going to rain on us today but partway through the morning, the clouds parted and the sun shone through. I told him that as a weather forecaster, he made a fabulous ballerina. The joke later turned on me.

Now as you enter the fringes of Astorga, you have a decision to make. Take the left turn off a roundabout or go straight on down a cul-de-sac. One or two pilgrims turned tail in the cul-de-sac and returned towards us. The ones who had taken the road waved their arms, imploring others to join them on that route. Dave, me and one or two other stubborn pilgrims ventured straight on. Ahead of us was a vivid green structure, maybe 400 yards at the end of the road. I can only describe it as a frame belonging to miniature rollercoaster. It still rose three storeys high though. As we approached, we saw that it was a metal framed walkway which took pedestrians over a railway track. Back and forth the green metal zig zagged. After traversing its length, we weren't so sure that it was indeed a shortcut.

Into the large town, heavy, grey clouds gathered, and the heavens opened on us as we struggled to find our Albergue. Ponchos on, the first time in many days, and into the historic centre. We were absolutely dripping wet. Just when an air of despondency set about us, wouldn't you know it, but the Camino smiled upon us. We were rounding a corner near the cathedral, and what an impressive sight that is, when we heard live music.

A band of minstrels in historic garb had filled a chocolate shop and were serenading the shoppers and staff with what I can only describe as "mariachi music". We took videos and photos. Sadly, I can only put a photo in the blog. It completely invigorated our flagging spirits and we smiled.

Our Albergue, some 400 yards away, via back alleys, is called "San Javier". A very old building, of at least 400 years. A friendly greeting from an older guy and then his son assisted in confirming our booking. Up a flight of rickety stairs and along an uneven timber floor to our dormitory. Five bunk beds in a room from a Charles Dickens novel. The floorboards in the dormitory above were already creaking with the footsteps of fellow pilgrims.

Showered and ready to explore Astorga, I gave the kitchen a quick once over. It will suffice for the culinary delights I have in mind.

We find one of the few bars that are open just around the corner from a Carrefour Express. How convenient is that! As we order our first food of the day, a hamburger, but what a hamburger, we are joined in the bar by one of the groups of minstrels. In my poor Spanish, I explain who we are and a little of what we were about. Subsequently, they are only too eager to pose for the customary photo before they press on to their next stop.

It's back to the Albergue for 6pm. It's that full that the "lounge area", in front of the roaring fire, is now laid out with mattresses and blankets. Pilgrims from all four corners of the world are here.

(Not a great photograph
but the back end of the pampered pooch from the passage below can be seen).

Following a "fake carbonara", as an Italian pilgrim called it, all jars and cheap processed meat, we drank the last of the wine and prepared ourselves for bed. The healthy portion of carbonara that was left we offered to a skinny German lad who apparently had no home but the Camino. He had his faithful dog, which had been fed by the owners of the Albergue, and not much else but what he carried. Apparently, he had the promise of a job in Hamburg in a couple of weeks' time. Here's hoping. He gratefully wolfed down our "fake carbonara". Post meal, I watched in amazement as he rubbed cream into his dog's paws with such tenderness. The faithful mutt clearly understood his master's kindness and licked the back of his attentive hands in supplication. It seems the poor pooch was suffering like the rest of us.

It's just gone 8pm and I'm in a bunk above Christine, who has a reet broad Northern accent. It transpires she's from Clitheroe. We were almost neighbours once, apart from 40 miles and the Lancashire Moors.

The Unnerving Crosses Don't Ward Off the Snow

Camino. Day 22. From Astorga to Rabanal Del Camino. 22k.
(Only 247k to Santiago).

Last night was not a good night in which you could catch up on your sleep. Not the pilgrims, but the residents of Astorga celebrating who knows what fiesta. Asleep before 9pm but woken at 10:30pm by several Spaniards on their way home from the local bars. This was followed by all the diverted traffic off the

M6 motorway, which miraculously had found its way from the UK and proceeded through the exceedingly narrow streets outside our dormitory. Just as this subsided, the German lad's dog began to bark downstairs. I'm not sure what troubled him, maybe the traffic, but it was now almost midnight. Finally, one lone party animal at God knows what o'clock, decided on serenading us at the top of his voice as he no doubt stumbled from wall to wall on each side of the cobbled road below.

I knew Dave had set his alarm for 6am and I heard him get up. We both got ready for the day and finally met downstairs in the foyer of this ancient building. It was now 06:10am. Dave had got up before the alarm and I didn't realise. The picture of the front of our Albergue is taken around this time.

We set off and after a very long five minutes we managed to find a cafe that was open so early on this Sunday morning. Maybe it had just finished serving the late-night fiesta shift.

It was a really cold morning with more rain forecast later, according to Rudolf Nureyev. After a short time, we saw a small "Ermita" chapel, which was open and ready to receive the pilgrims. We walked through Murias de Rechivieldo and on to Santa Catalina de Samoza. It was a gentle, lengthy climb and quite enjoyable in the chill, first light of day. Bright yellow broom all alongside the path with verdant, green forests all around. A good time to be alive, irrespective of the lack of sleep. We approached Santa Catalina de Samoza with a spring in our step. We had been in each other's company all morning. Life is good. Just as we entered the village, the first cafe/taverna was open to our righthand side. What a lovely place. It is called El Camineza. It was a picture. We both said that if we had known of its existence, then we may have pushed on to stay the night here. For anyone else who is considering this pilgrimage, do yourself a favour and look it up. As we enjoyed our coffee and banana, we noticed an older, stout man with his much younger, nubile female "partner". They were completely blotto and ordered two more bottles of beer as we tried not to watch their antics. They must have been at it, I mean drinking, all night. Maybe they were some of the revellers from last night, who knows?

We had completed 10k by now and had a further 12k to do. The scenery and walking were so much better here than the last week or so. Up out of town and climbing continually for some 8k. Thankfully, it wasn't too steep; that comes tomorrow and later in the week. The foothills before the mountains continued with their lush vegetation, so many hues of green around us as the forests spread to the horizon. It was a pleasure. No constantly looking down at your feet here. The next village was El Ganso. We decided to split up the last few kilometres and settled for another brew in "The Cowboy Bar". Phone put on charge, as always when the opportunity arises. Strangely enough, a vacant plug socket is the first thing you look for when you arrive at a watering hole. Up through another wooded area that was completely dead. A metal fence along the path, which ran for several hundred meters, was full of crosses made from that dead wood, other material or anything the previous pilgrims could lay their hands on. Personally, I found it to be quite unnerving. Then I heard the sound of another twig being snapped from a dead tree behind me. Another cross to weigh the fence down.

Our Albergue was only a few hundred meters ahead and was called La Senda. We were greeted by an elderly gentleman called Matteo. The place was spotless, the bathrooms clean with hot, strong showers and blankets already waiting on the beds. Laundry service and a roaring fire upstairs in the salon with a small but adequate kitchen next door. For five euros we couldn't fault it.

As I write this blog, Dave and I are sat in a bar called El Tesin, which adjoins our Albergue. Dave has rushed outside to take a video and photo as IT'S SNOWING! We knew it was cold but blimey. Matteo had better get more blankets out.

Up to the local shop, two tins of lentils, bread and blue cheese.

We tried to have a siesta prior to shopping but it wasn't long before four young Germans came in. Their spirits high along with their laughter and banter. We gave up trying to sleep and went back next door to the bar. What else could one do? As we enjoyed the hospitality of El Tesin, we watched the intrepid pilgrims traipse past in the falling snow. Sam from America, a young German lad and Joanne from New Zealand passed the bar, and we ran outside to greet them. They were pressing on to the next town, God bless them.

They were followed by a German lady called Regina, pronounced Regeena! We had bumped into her briefly in the last few days. She asked us where we were staying, and I pointed out the Albergue and gave her a brief synopsis re price and cleanliness. Off she trotted through the Albergue door and booked her bunk. She joined us a short while later in the bar. We drank and laughed for an hour or so. She is a delight. Apparently, she lives in the Birmingham area of the UK and is married to an English man whom she plans to meet in Santiago. We will see Regina most days of the remaining Camino.

We'd spent sufficient time in the bar and so set off up the cobbled street to a small grocer on the left. The fields to our right now had a light dusting of snow. We purchased our food and set off to the kitchen in our Albergue. Although it may not sound appetising but tea was lovely. Blue cheese and fresh bread for starters and the tins of lentils, which had chorizo in, was supplemented by pasta and all was washed down with a cheap bottle of plonk. Small chocolate sponge squares rescued from yesterday finished us off. For you would-be pilgrims reading this, it really is part of the fun, making so many lovely acquaintances, roughing it and making the most of everything that comes your way.

This is Regina.

Yes, she too signed the T-shirt.

Tears for Dad

Camino. Day 23. From Rabanal Del Camino to Molinaseca. 29k.
(592K in Total).

Well, it was a better night's sleep than we expected, following the disturbed afternoon siesta. Stepping out of the Albergue door, we immediately felt the chill run through our bones. First decision of the day, out with the thermal socks and get my hands covered quickly just like wearing a pair of kids' mittens. I was only missing the long cord, which would hold them together to thread through my sleeves and around my back. It had snowed a little more overnight, which had now frozen and crunched underfoot. Up the hill to our left and climb, climb, climb. It started to snow again, fine ice crystals filled the air. It was really quite invigorating. The foliage, either side of the path, glistened and bowed slightly with the weight of the snow and frost. There were some lovely purple bushes all around us now as we ascended. I can only liken them to "lanky heather". It was a magical time to be walking the Camino and we soon warmed up as the ground came up to meet our feet quicker as we rose into the pine forests and on onwards the village of Foncebadon some six kilometres away. Maybe the Christmas reindeer on the windowsill a couple of days ago wasn't out of season after all.

The last few hundred meters to the village were along the roadside. The wind had picked up and the snow, which by now was considerably heavier, was driven into us by a biting gale. The excess snow from the roadside was being whipped up into snow serpents, which wound around our boots and gaiters (when packing, I thought that the gaiters may have been an unnecessary item but boy they were worth their weight in gold).

The cafe came up on our left. It was so welcome. Other pilgrims who had stayed in this village also took refuge in this warm, bright oasis before they too ventured out into what was becoming a blizzard. We were served by an Italian lady who said that she was from the south of Italy when I enquired about her accent. I looked outside and she followed my gaze into the flurrying snow. My eyes went back to hers and I smiled.

I said, 'You must be here for love?'

She too smiled, but coyly. She stated that she had come to Spain for the love of the Camino, but yes, she had found her true love en route and had settled here some two years before.

Half an hour later and reluctant to leave this cosy nook, we took a deep breath and stepped out into the ever-increasing blizzard. Still climbing on up to a height of 1,450 meters. It's the highest point on the whole Camino. All well and good, but the view wasn't up to much as we couldn't see more than 200 yards in front of us. Before we knew it, things were compounded, as we had reached the cloud line and I for one began to feel a little uneasy.

Dave commented, 'I bet it's lovely here in May!'

He paused, smiled at me and then said, 'Oh, that's tomorrow!'

He then shouted my name. I turned, and he threw a snowball at me. Finally, we came upon the Ermita de Santiago and the Cruz de Ferro. The chapel was closed but just in front of it was the 50-foot-high cross, which is surrounded by a mound comprising hundreds of thousands of stones left there by pilgrims. Each stone represents a burden they wished to unload or have come to terms with. Apparently, some of these stones have been carried on very, very long journeys.

Dave captured my approach to the Cruz.

I had found a set of wooden rosary beads with a crucifix attached. I knew the instant I picked them up on one of my training days, near Rebate, exactly where it was meant to rest forever. I climbed the snow-covered stones with some difficulty; they were treacherous. I tied the rosary beads and crucifix to the cross.

It now had my sisters name, "Ann"; my name "Steve", along with the words "For Dad" written on the back of the crucifix. I said a prayer for all of the people I had known, who sadly had now departed this world. Some recent family, people I had genuinely got to love, ex-colleagues and friends. Blimey, this Camino gets into your veins and tugs remorselessly at every heartstring.

I suspect that Dave had moments of reverence here too. Photos taken and off again downhill. It's still snowing but not as bad as before. The blizzard was being held off by the pine forest we entered into for a while.

It was a long way to the next stop. However, around a bend, what I can only describe as three, single-storey, ramshackle barns stood together. This was apparently Monjardin. It was full of oddments hanging from its walls and rickety tables. A log fire was burning outside the entrance, but the prevailing wind merely sent the smoke inside temporarily filling the barns, before it escaped through the large gaps in the old, wooden walls. It reeked. The trinkets offered to the pilgrims were scattered around and a placed amongst them were two, self-dispensing thermos flasks filled with tepid, and I suspect, old coffee.

We declined and turned tail back onto the road. If it wasn't for the 21st century clothing and equipment worn by us all, I would suggest that the scene before us looked like something from the dark ages or a stage set from earlier Blackadder episodes. Sadly, we still had a further eight kilometres to walk before we reached El Acebo. The conditions underfoot were so terrible at this point. We had now left the tarmac, which was boring, but we were now stumbling down, steep, rocky paths with loose rocks and stones giving away underfoot.

Aching and hungry, we plodded into El Acebo. Wow! What a place. Sorry to say, this but it was another film set, this time from Ivanhoe or some similar genre. Narrow streets, old wooden balconies, which were twisted with age and decay that almost separated themselves from the main buildings and fell to the cobbles below.

Hunger beset us as we entered a cafe bar. We ordered a hearty helping of eggs, pork loin and potatoes with a side order of bread. We chose a table next to a radiator and huddled close to it. Our next stretch of the day was a further eight kilometres, via two more villages. One which was called Ambos was lovely.

Outside one particular house was a tree covered in pale yellow blossom. It resembled popcorn. Absolutely beautiful, I'd never seen this type of tree before. Almost immediately, everything went downhill, literally and metaphorically. The paths became horrendous, probably the worst we had encountered so far.

For several kilometres, all we could do was take "baby steps", barely covering the ground at half a boot's length at a time.

We had taken time to look back at the mountains we had just travelled through just a few short hours before. They were still shrouded by the stormy snow clouds. I have to say that at this point, I am immensely proud of Dave and myself. Whilst you're ticking off the points of interest on your travels, you simply don't appreciate the achievement until you take time to look back on yourself. The next picture shows exactly what I mean. I cannot begin to understand the feeling real explorers get, who climb Everest or force their bodies to endure trips to the North or South Poles. By the way, I'm not even comparing ourselves to those heroes, but the picture below shows just what a hard day it had been for two portly old mates. It was bloody awesome for us.

Some two hours later at almost 2 o'clock in the afternoon, Molinaseca appeared shortly before we approached the road. It was lovely and the inviting view across the Rio Borazon simply enhanced the picturesque view, probably the best town on the Camino thus far.

Wouldn't you know it, our Albergue was at the far end of the town yet again. It was called Santa Marina. A huge Swiss style cottage of a building, which was almost new inside and quite modern. Hoorah, single beds, proper beds, in a ten-bed dormitory. Sadly, it's on the second floor and the showers and toilets are in the basement. Bizarre. Who the hell designs these places?

Ready and back into town just to stretch our legs and maybe risk a couple of cheeky beers, a light snack and back for some well-earned rest. Post-beer, we decided to buy some bread, ham, cheese, chocolate and water, yes water, from a store. We snuck our goodies back into the Albergue under our jackets just like two naughty schoolboys at boarding school. We did this as the hosts provided a pilgrim's menu but at 15 euros per head, this was a little too steep, even for our pockets. My towel laid out on the bed like a picnic rug, I set about making a blinking large butty. The dorms were empty now. Another day over and it's not even 8pm.

Boiling Cauldrons

Day 24. Molinaseca to Cacabelos. 24k. (Only 188k to Santiago).

Getting up early is becoming a habit for both of us. Into the basement just after 6am for a wash, etc, and we take our rucksacks with us to save disturbing the other pilgrims. The front door to the Albergue was locked but we managed to escape via the boot room and back garden at 06:35am. Socks for gloves again and hood up to keep the warmth in once we had picked up a steady pace. It takes a few hundred metres for the aching joints and feet to readapt. Into the little but quaint village of Campo on the outskirts of Ponferrada. There are flowers all along the paths and in the gardens. They are the most noticeable things here, down in the dells from the mountain tops around us. Red poppies, purple iris, lavender and wisteria. Yellows, whites and deep purples from others we did not recognise. Then white clematis and marigolds. Alan Titchmarsh, eat your heart out. The mountains we had climbed the day before were lit by the rising sun. We spent many minutes looking to our left at this scene. It was absolutely stunning and satisfying. I really don't know what mountaineers in the Himalayas must go through. We were exhilarated.

Next stop, Ponferrada. Initially a quite uninviting town but once inside, boy, it's lovely. Hot tea/coffee and some of our pilgrim friends join us. The castle and old town, shown in the pictures, are just across the road.

It was a lovely 50 minutes' walk through Ponferrada, via a bank and chemist, before we rose again and up through the hamlets of Columbrianos and Fuentes Nuevas. This was a lovely day and lovely place to be walking through. The countryside was beautiful. The paths full of friendly, happy pilgrims and the air about us was full of joy. Camponaraya next. We stopped for a few minutes on a bench. Dave ate a chocolate cake from the previous night, whilst I finished off my ham, cheese and tomato baguette (soggy, to say the least). Off once again but with brief and very steep climbs. One of them only a few hundred meters long but absolutely tortuous. I trudged forward and passed a woman who was meandering from one side of the path to another, just to take the incline out of it. She did, however, make it four times longer. I turned around to see that Dave had now adopted the same method. He doesn't take kindly to hills, does our Dave.

Just 3k short of Cacabelos was an impromptu stop. A caravan, awning tied to a tree and a fruit smoothie with my name on it. Dave had a coke but whilst I was getting the drinks, Dave was buying a Camino Scallop Shell for me. He is amazing. He is unflustered, generous, considerate and a fabulous mate to have by your side.

The 3k into Cacabelos was unremarkable with the exception that the patchouli oil, worn by many younger pilgrims, was beginning to fill the air. Apparently, it's to mask the body odour of the less clean pilgrims but it seemed to be getting stronger by the day. Their hygiene was clearly not up to our standards, as low as ours were. As we neared the town, everything changed. Cars parked everywhere, traffic, hustle and bustle of people. It was May Day, with a market day and a fiesta for the village. It was just what two weary pilgrims needed to pick them up. It was vibrant. Via the narrow street and throngs of people, grandparents, children, aunts, uncles and young teenagers. Our Albergue, La Gallega, appeared on the righthand side of the throng. It was pleasant enough. We are sharing an intimately small room with Jos and Titia from the Netherlands. En suite shower and bathroom. Really nice.

Outside and into the sun. I will not bore you with my telecommunication problems at this stage. I was starving and just across the small street a sign to warm the cockles of a poor pilgrims heart, "Doner Kebab"! Who am I to fly in the face of fate? It was not the best I've ever had but it was the most needed. Dave, bless him, resisted. Off we went through the narrow streets to explore and just around the corner was the market. It was still in full swing. It was bouncing! We meandered through the stalls. Dave had settled, mentally at least, to having a bocadillo of some description. Then, there it was. A queue of people waiting, maybe 20 of them. An umbrella, clouds of condensation and two women serving the throng as quickly as they could. The steam was coming from one of two huge cauldrons, which were bubbling away. We both salivated as a man walked away with a huge plate of the delicacy and a baguette. OCTOPUS! Plates in three sizes. Steaming hot octopus covered in olive oil, paprika and salt. I found a table at a nearby bar and bought the wine in preparation. I took a glass to Dave whilst he waited in line. In truth, I had forgotten I'd had the doner kebab or I just didn't care. I returned to our table with its wine and filled glass to find an elderly Spanish gentleman and his grandson sat there, about to relieve me of my Camino spoils. I was none too happy, and my tone rather than my limited Spanish evicted them. Dave arrived with the hot goods. I have to ask myself if anything has ever tasted better at this moment, certainly not the kebab. People all around us were bringing steaming plates of it to their tables at the various bars around us. The landlords clearly didn't care. It was an octopus festival.

The whole atmosphere captivated us and so, in true Dave and Steve tradition, we drank several rounds more. It just seemed to be the right thing to do. Back from the excitement of the market, it's 7:00pm. Just time for a coffee and brandy before retiring to our boudoir. The streets outside our Albergue are still crammed with thousands of May Day revellers. What a place, what a day, what a Camino!

Time to Stop and Laugh at Quilters' Cabin

Camino. Day 25. From Cacabelos to Vega de Valcarce. 25k.

We were awoken by the sound of Titia announcing that it was 6am, a time we had all agreed we would get up and be able to put the light on without fear of upsetting somebody. Morning ablutions completed and downstairs, where, to my surprise, two ladies were waiting in the adjoining bar to serve morning coffee. How very convivial. We made the most of it as this was the first time in many days that we had the opportunity to have a hot drink before venturing out into the cold.

In truth, it wasn't too cold when we finally set foot on the street. Cool, yes but no need for glove-socks. The Camino took us out of town through an incredible amount of rubbish still left on the streets, in the bushes and in the river, from the market yesterday. Quite a disappointment, as the Spanish usually clean the streets post fiesta/market immediately. However, we realised that yesterday was in fact Labour Day and perhaps even the street cleaners get this day off. Somewhat of an "oxymoron" on this occasion.

Yet again we climbed, although today was different in so much as our route seemed to be snaking around in every conceivable direction. At some points, we even thought we were going around in circles. Through Pieros and out towards Villafranca Del Biergo, it was eight kilometres door to door before a break. How many times on this part of the Camino did we question whether it was the right path, as there were few, if any, markers. Having come off the road, we came across a yard full of, well, stone figures, Horses' heads, obscure poles and statues. The gate was padlocked but we reckon it was a sculptor's yard.

Obligatory photo taken, we moved on and into the deep valley, which secluded Villafranca from the world. We noticed during the descent that the temperature fell by a few degrees. It was chilly to say the least before we entered a welcome cafe.

As we entered Villafranca Del Biergo, I saw a sign on a renovated barn wall. I nearly collapsed. I found myself laughing out loud, which Dave clearly could not understand. This is why.

In the late 1990s, I was posted as a detective sergeant to Longsight in Greater Manchester. My team comprised of DC Ian Graham, DC Marie Phelan and a trainee called Simon Quartermaine, (ex-Met Police). We were on 3/11 shift. Ian, Simon and I were sat at a bank of computers, updating our crimes or checking what was going on in the force. Marie was at her desk, completing yet another prosecution file. Ian found something on his screen, to his dislike. To this day, I don't know what it was. He set off in a hissy fit and used the very bad 'C' word out loud. Now, Marie was an extraordinary woman, but that particular word clearly pissed her right off. She bawled at Ian, took no prisoners and let him know that in no uncertain terms was he to use that particular word ever again. Simon and I put on our tin hats and hid under the desk. An uneasy calm beset the office until five minutes later, Ian let out yet another outburst which ended off with the words "You Quilt!", clearly to appease Marie. Simon and I burst out laughing and the "Quilt" word stuck, it still does. Marie smiled, battle won and point clearly made.

Forward my life, probably 20 years. One evening, out with friends at a pub quiz. For the first time, we were struggling to think of a team name until it came to me like a flash of lightning, "The Four Quilts"! Well, who would know? I smirked. They all knew something deep in my mind was about to flower right in front of them. I recounted the Longsight story to the team, and it was agreed. Furthermore the demure, glamorous and very Irish Lena leant forward and beckoned the group into a huddle to hear her syrupy, Irish drawl, whisper a joke. It went like this…

Little Girl: 'Mummy, Mummy, Mummy.'
Mother: 'Yes, darling?'
Little Girl: 'What's a penis?'
Mother: 'Oh, darling, you know when you have a bath with Daddy?'
Little Girl: 'Yes.'
Mother: 'Well, when he stands up to get dried, it's that dangly thing between his legs.'

Now satisfied with the answer, but still perplexed, the little girl continued.

Little Girl:　'Well, Mummy, then what's a cunt?'
Mother:　　　'Oh, darling. That's just the rest of him!'

Subsequently, the photo I took of the poster for "Quilters Cabin" took me to another time and place completely. Dave now understands.

On through Villafranca, we tried to take the quick road out of town. We asked an old gentleman if we were right, but he turned us around, as pilgrims or anyone else on foot couldn't use the road which went through a tunnel. It had no footpath and was subsequently dangerous. We now set off via the rest of the picturesque town and out along the road, which constantly wound to and fro between hills and through gorges. However, before we left the town, something beset me. It was weird. I found myself craving, and I mean CRAVING chocolate. I wanted it NOW. For God's sake, the Camino has got me pregnant! An open store 50 yards ahead, a telling off from the assistant for entering with my rucksack (clearly an archetypal shoplifter, if there was ever one in these parts), but thankfully the chocolate was straight in front of me. I snatched the two biggest bars I could see, paid the assistant and tore the wrapping off one with my teeth whilst offering the second bar to Dave. Gone in seconds, my craving satiated, I skipped on.

I can only liken Villafrance Del Biergo to being in North Wales, Betws-y-Coed, to be precise. We meandered out of town with the sides of the gorge towering above us. Just ahead were Regina and another female. They were picking something from the hedgerow at the side of the footpath. It was dill. Fresh, very green and tasty. There was lots of it. We exchanged pleasantries and off we went with the river Valcarce running alongside us. It was in full flow and absolutely crystal clear.

After a few kilometres, we caught up with two pilgrims known to us. Joanne the Kiwi and Gilles the Canadian. We walked together for a short while before our natural pace took us away from them. It was another 10k before we stopped for a bite to eat in a tiny hamlet called Trabadelo. The cafe had a huge and seemingly old bar inside, the front of which was an exquisitely carved mural of pilgrims walking the Camino.

The next picture is at the end of the village and shows the historic decay on the Camino. It's everywhere and I will debate this more towards the end of my account.

As we left the café, we saw the Italian lad, Hercules, we hadn't seen him since Day Two. We smiled and shook hands. He remembered us and said that he didn't think we would have made it this far. First impressions, eh! The last time he had seen us we had stopped, puffing and panting, halfway up a hill. Maybe it had been our impressive physical appearance, on which he had come to this conclusion. Perversely, we thought the same of him in reverse.

Anyway, on via Pereje, Ambasmistas and finally under an incredible feat of engineering, ie the roadway, some several hundred feet above us, which spanned a gorge, we entered Vega Del Valcarce. We had initially booked beds in the Albergue Magdalena, but this place was the absolute pits. It made the railway sidings at Fromista with Tom, Dick and Harry look like five-star luxury. The stench of mould and God knows what else was awful. You have been warned! We turned tail and went back to a beautiful Albergue, Sarracin. It had lovely pictures on its roadside. The hoarding boards showed pictures of steaks with new potatoes. It was full and we hadn't made a reservation. Back again into the village, we visited another promising but full Albergue. Surely we weren't destined to sleep in the world's worst Albergue? Fortunately, the owner of the premises in which we stood made a phone call to Maria, her sister. She just happened to own the "Pension Fernandez" a couple of hundred meters away. What a stroke of luck. We were greeted by the loveliest lady on the whole Camino. A smile, so helpful and she escorted us to our twin room, which was better than those of the hotels we have stayed in. Luck was clearly on our side at this moment. The view from our room was simply wonderful. A raging torrent of a river, field, hills and an old guy fly fishing for trout.

Hot shower, changed and into town to buy tea. Tuna salad on the menu tonight. As we shopped, we bumped into the Kiwi, Joanne. We had walked with her for a few hundred meters earlier. At that point, she had been with the Canadian, Gilles. He had a problem with his Achilles and now she was on her own and moving on. She had just stopped off at Albergue Sarracin for lunch. Butternut soup, followed by fresh trout. She tried to tell us just how good it had been, she had us from the start of her recollection. We were salivating.

Groceries bought, a snack and a beer and back to our lovely, cozy, warm room.

At this point, I have to point out that I have virtually lost contact with the outside world. Between EE and Apple, they have completely messed up, and I could have said much worse with my iPhone. It is of no use whatsoever, I can't even take photos on it. I will not bore you with the technical details, but I can't get it sorted until Santiago, where I have to find an Apple Store. I'm livid, to put it mildly. Subsequently, the photos I've taken today of Villafranca and elsewhere do not appear. My mate and brother pilgrim, Dave is credited with what follows and will be probably until the end of the Camino.

Fed and watered, tuna salad and wine, we are off to sleep early as we can't get football on our TV and it's a very big day ahead, which has the last mountain, or two, or three, of the Camino. Three to four hours of "climbing up a step ladder" ahead of us on the first mountain alone. Night night our lovely friends and sponsors.

Hibernating Grizzly Bear Cubs with Fat, Round Bellies

Camino. Day 26. From Vega De Valcarce to Fonfria. (26.25k).

Today was a day when Dave and I achieved a number of significant moments.

First, I again have to mention Pension Fernandez. It's simply the best place we have stayed. The breakfast room had assorted cakes, bread, cereals, waffles, honey, fruit, juice and more. We just had tea and hot chocolate but took a couple of cakes for later. Dave completed the "guests' comments" book with a glowing tribute.

Out into the cool, still, morning. The damp in the air held by the deep gorge in which Valcarce lies. We had only walked a few hundred yards when we spotted a deer to our right. I have attached a photo. The deer is dead centre, but you may not quite make it out. You will just have to take my word.

A gentle climb and just to our right a staggering piece of engineering. Two more roads cross a wide valley supported by concrete pillars several hundred feet high. Each piece of the span, and there were many, must have been 100 meters in length. We just cannot comprehend the technology, planning, design and construction that it's taken to build these mammoth structures. I'm sure my sons will explain over a beer one day, as this is their field of expertise.

It was all going so well but we knew what lay ahead. Six kilometres done and then we turned left. It reared up in front of us. Hell's bells! This was a steep one. The broken rock path through the woods. The first day is reputedly the hardest climb, maybe because you haven't worn in your Camino legs or just because of the height and distance but the gradient on this, the O'Cerbriero climb, was around one in three and we knew it went on for over 5k.

We reached La Faba, a tiny hamlet part way up. Time to stop for ten minutes at an ancient building that held a cafe within. We really needed to stop as often as possible today. We were served by a cool guy with dreadlocks and relaxing music played. We chose homemade muesli biscuits to fortify ourselves. Back out and into the cold air. It takes a few minutes to warm up when your top and the inside of your coat are wringing wet with sweat. It helped the chill eat into your bones until your blood gets pumping again.

We are climbing up through the clouds now and the valleys stretch out below us in several directions. The edges of the "paths" are an explosion of yellow, primroses, broom and what I can only describe as tiny daffodils.

Three Italian women are taking photos of themselves as they stand in front of a purple "Lanky Heather" bush. We approach and I see one of them pick up a dead branch which had fallen from the bush. She started to sweep the path, as if it were a broom. I asked her permission, took it from her and placed it between my legs and said, 'Bruja.'

She said, 'Si, broom.'

I smiled and cheekily said, 'Witch.'

This, she and her friends understood and giggled. She said, 'Maybe I can fly up then,' in perfect English.

If only it were that easy.

This is one hell of a climb and we took a further break at Laguna de Castilla. I'd just heard a farmer tell a Spanish Pilgrim, who was a few yards ahead, that there were still two kilometres to the top. The peak is 1,330 meters, or 4,364 feet. That's just 15 meters less than the height of Ben Nevis. However, before we reached there, the first achievement came as we passed a marker post which declared that we were now in Galicia! As you can see, it's sadly been defaced, something I don't quite understand, especially from pilgrims.

I don't know what was in the muesli cookies but we bounced on. Sadly, from a pictorial point, there was no stunning view from the top as we were still engulfed in cloud. There was, however, a photo opportunity right in front of us. A statue of a woman sat serenely down on the edge of a wall. Sponsored T-shirts out, and for health reasons, they were worn outside our coats. We were simply frozen to the core.

213

Just off to the right was a collection of stone buildings with domed roofs. They were hundreds of years old. One contained a gift shop, the other a cafe. Time to replenish our depleted stamina with a large slice of tuna and tomato empanada and a hot drink. I took a photo inside just because of the age of these buildings.

Dave and I had done it! Or so we thought. Off we skipped, well not quite, but briefly it was downhill and only another 12 kilometres to Fonfria.

All of a sudden, we climbed yet again, back up to 1,270 meters, with a large statue of a pilgrim marking this peak.

Down again and then the big surprise, one of which we had not been informed by a mate who had walked the Camino three times. It was yet another climb up to Alto de Poyo. At 1,337 meters, it's higher than O'Cerbriero. Our lungs were bursting by now and I could hear the blood rushing through the veins around my head and ears. Sweat was pouring out of every blinking pore. An Australian guy was stood at the top of this climb on the patio of a closed cafe. He engaged me in conversation, but my replies were somewhat of a staccato nature with a gentle wheeze. Surely Fonfria must be around the corner? No, another 3k. A kilometre from the Albergue our final achievement. A marker post showed 149k to Santiago. Hopefully by Wednesday?

The Albergue is called Reboliera. We were greeted by "Daniel", who took our nine euros, stamped our Camino passport and escorted us to our dormitory. There were 17 sets of bunk beds, but it was spotless. Right now, I don't care if there are a thousand pilgrims sleeping around me tonight.

The picture with the view of a distant hill with a blue sky, has just been taken from inside our Albergue. It's 5:45pm and although it looks lovely, it is cold.

It's the pilgrim's menu tonight, nine euros, but we have to walk across the road to the dining area.

There were 30-odd of us in the round, thatched barn, which looked centuries old. The tables were laid out and there were bottles of water and wine all over them. A sumptuous salad, followed by piles of beautiful, tender beef, which had been lovingly cooked in a sauce with red peppers. It was served with boiled rice. It was simply fabulous and there was enough of it for several helpings each. The wine was guzzled by all and as each bottle was emptied, it was instantly replaced by a full one. Sometimes you just have to realise that enough is enough and remember what the next day brings.

Just like young grizzly bears with full round stomachs, we set off to hibernate, well, for a few hours anyway.

Let the Conspiracy Theory Begin

Camino. Day 27. From Fonfria to Sarria (34k)

It's one degree outside as we leave the Albergue. It had not been a good night for sleeping in a dormitory with so many beds. In particular, one young woman who occupied the bed between the exit door and men's toilet door, not a good choice, I may add, was clearly practising for the World Snoring Championships (snorking, as our friends from the Netherlands call it).

We follow the main road for a short while. Flat and uneventful. Our minds should have been switched on, what were we thinking? Following yesterday's dramatic climb, there had to be an enormous descent and here it was. The knee jarring, leg aching, fall to the valleys below. It was painful and long, taking away a little of the satisfaction that we achieved yesterday. Regina later commented that it had almost reduced her to tears. Don't get me wrong, the paths on the whole were well maintained, it was just kilometre after kilometre of pain. Dave, with his tightening calves and me with my right knee, which has had me walking like "Keyser Soze" from the film The Usual Suspects, since Day Two. The woods and fields and other scenery passed in a blur until we reached Tricastela, some 13 kilometers from our first stop of the day. Fields like an embroidered, patchwork, quilt came into view. So many different shades of green. The Spanish version of drystone walling on display. Not as intricate or indeed well made but sturdy and rustic. Tricastela was a lovely town, picturesque and vibrant, buzzing with pilgrims all searching for the mid-morning pick-me-up. Onwards and upwards. Another steep climb, over the top and onto Furela. 24 kilometres done, eight more to do and boy was everything aching. As the time passed, the temperature rose and we found ourselves with just one top on, with our sodden coats wrapped away in our rucksacks. Gently downhill now into the large town of Sarria. We were staying in the Monastery Magdalena. Yes, it was in the far side of town, yes, it was up another hill, yes, it was another dormitory of 30 beds, but boy, what a welcome sight.

As we waited outside, Lilly joined us, and we chatted for a while. Suddenly, I felt something land on my neck. I swiftly reached up, grabbed the offending insect, opened my hand to release it unharmed but looked down before it flew off. It was a bee. Off it went, leaving its sting implanted at the base of my left, middle, finger. Sadly, it will die now. I can't recall being stung before. Other pilgrims we knew joined us.

As well as Lilly from Norway, there was Marvin, from Germany. We settled into our dormitory in the monastery and set off to explore the town. Some of the old, historic buildings had been engulfed by the modern era cement buildings, with a function rather than an architectural beauty. The older buildings were lovely, regal and statesman like in comparison.

Dave and I found a Spanish/Italian cafe-bar. We dined on a lovely, multi stack hamburger with a cool beer. The warm sun turned the courtyard, in which we sat, to the cosiest little spot. We could quite easily have nodded off, but it was time to move on, explore a little and purchase groceries for tea, which I would be cooking later in the monastery kitchen. Lilly had left us and had gone to find a doctor. Her feet and legs were extremely sore and she was having difficulty walking any distance at all.

Late afternoon, Dave and I had bought our food and settled down at a bar on the narrow street leading up to our monastery. We intended having a little aperitif and taking in the last of the spring sun. Our seats were on the footpath just up from the Albergue Obradoiro, and we set about people watching and planning our return from Finisterre. Albergue Obradoiro was fascinating, as through the open front door you could see a hallway lined with a seven-foot-high wooden panel, which had been completely carved with images of pilgrims and other religious figures. It ran the length of the hallway.

We were joined after a short while by Sam from America, Marvin, Regina and Gilles. The "aperitif" was about to turn into an outrageous and hilarious session. Before it disintegrated, however, Lilly appeared. It was bad news. She had found a doctor, who had informed her that she had shin splints and an ankle problem. She will have to finish the Camino by bus and says she will stop at every town to join up with those she knows, particularly Marvin from Germany. As we reminisced about our journey, the conversation became deep and serious, almost conspiratorial. We discussed the true meaning of the pilgrimage, Christianity, the decay in the Spanish heritage, the money we had spent and where it, in turn, was being utilised, particularly in relation to the Camino. We started to question everything about this pilgrimage, and I will go into greater detail at the end of my diaries. Sam talked about a Spanish Priest named Elijah Valina Sampedro, who had been the pastor at O'Cebriero and one of the most important figures in the revival of the modern pilgrimage to Santiago. Further research from Debbie revealed that when Valina started promoting the ancient route, some parts were impassable. After convincing mayors, other parishes and associations to become involved, the task of marking the original route began between the late 1970s and 1980s. Don Elias created the yellow arrows that the hundreds of thousands of pilgrims now follow to Santiago. The whiff of conspiracy and back handers has entered my nostrils!

After a couple of hours' debate Dave and I were asked what we were doing for tea. We showed them the groceries and a couple set off to the supermarket a few hundred yards away to supplement our provisions. We drank and dined together. I cooked salmon, new potatoes and asparagus for the main course, with bread and blue cheese for starters. Seven of us ate together. It was lovely. Nine o'clock came upon us and it's time for bed. Earplugs in and off to sleep for a short while. The dormitory filled up with new faces. They were the "Frog Chorus" throughout the night, due to the variety of snoring tones from almost every bed. It transpires that these frogs are the new pilgrims who only "Walk" the last 100 kilometres to get their twice daily stamps, in exchange for their Compostela/certificate on arrival in Santiago de Compostela in less than a week's time.

Today, late afternoon, the plans Dave and I had suffered a terminal blow. We were booking all of the Albergues in advance now that we knew we would arrive in Santiago DC by Wednesday. Places would be scarce now the hundreds of newbies had joined us. Dave and I had set a further three days to walk to

Finisterre, which contains some of the most beautiful scenery on the whole Camino. We set about booking our flights, which, six weeks ago were 27 euros on Ryanair. To our complete dismay, they were now 224 euros each for a one-way trip lasting one hour 30 minutes. We simply could not afford this outrageous amount which had gone up eightfold. It had to be said that other airlines were the same price or dearer. No matter how we tried to reconfigure the dates, the costs were simply outrageous. We looked at car hire, other dates for flights, coaches, taxis at 130 euros from Finisterre to Santiago airport, every conceivable way was simply too much, and in our minds, completely unjustifiable. Maybe Michael O'Leary had eyes on the ground who tell him that this year in particular the Camino was absolutely crammed with pilgrims. Whispers seemed to be saying there were record numbers for this time of year.

I'm sorry to inform our family, friends, followers and supporters, that both Dave and I have come to the following decision. We will walk to Santiago de Compostela with our heads held high. That is the completion of the Camino Frances. On to Finisterre is the Camino de Finisterre. We will take a coach Thursday morning from Santiago to Finisterre. It costs just 6 euros each and is direct (sadly, it doesn't stop at Santa Marina, two days' walk post Santiago. If it had have done well, maybe we could have walked to Finisterre from there but it simply wasn't doable). So, we will get the coach, walk the last three kilometres to the very end of Finisterre and then back to the town. Stay one night in an Albergue before coaching it back to the airport for a further six euros and hopping on a 92 euro flight. I can't begin to tell you just how disappointed we both are. Thank you, Michael O'Leary and other airline operators.

Dave's Foot Massager, Complete with a Beaming Smile

Camino. Day 28. Sarria to Portomarin. (24.5k).

Well, our Couch Pilgrims what a different day it's been today.

Awake early due to the previously mentioned Frog Chorus. Pilgrims from all over the place trying to be quiet but not achieving it. Excited chatter from the "New Pilgrims" seemingly from the United States, Far East and Germany. We pack in a rush and get out by 06:45am. We are not the first on the Camino by any stretch of the imagination. Yet again, it's cold but the weather forecast tells us it should reach 71 degrees Fahrenheit later. We'd better crack on. The countryside has calmed down, although there's a sharp ascent after half an hour that brings sweat pouring out of our heads and bodies. Topping out, we pant to get our breath and sweep off down the path which runs through some of the most beautiful scenery of the Camino to date. Long horned, red cows, donkeys, stunning rolling hills covered in meadows of long, lush, grass which adorned it. Long yellow buttercups, purple, red and pink flowers compete for the sunlight as they peep above the blades of grass. It is absolutely stunning and both Dave and I have our spirits lifted. Coffee stop at 5k. We have walked with two ladies from South Carolina. It's their first day. One of them has stopped for breath four times already. Her mate is none too impressed. The paths are full of the new pilgrims. Yes, I know that it's THEIR Camino too and we have been warned to be tolerant. They are giddy, noisy, with unsullied boots, and bright colourful garb. They have sent their luggage on to their next destination, so they don't have the horrible burden of carrying it, God forbid (flaming Hell, they're only doing 100k)! They're in groups, chattering away with their expensive cameras, zoom lens attached and ready to snap at anything and I mean anything, even a bale of hay in a farmer's yard. Where have they been all their lives... Tolerant, be tolerant.

I concentrate on the wildlife. Kites, buzzards, buntings but I will have to research which ones. Then I spot a blue tit as it comes out of a tree. I pause and wait for its mate to enter the hole. I manage to creep to within five feet, Dave and two French ladies close behind, and we all see the second bird emerge from its nest, where there must be young. Several kilometres further on and maybe 6k from Portomarin, there's a rest stop. What a beautiful place. A break in a slate wall and onto a patio covered with clean white tables, chairs and parasols, it's called Mercadoiro.

The small shop across the way, serving Santiago cake, (soon to become Dave's favourite Camino delicacy), and other sweet delights, along with tuna and meat empanadas. Dave has cake and I have the meat empanada. Both with coffee. One guy, and it's not even 12 midday, has a pint of beer and a plate of octopus. The stunning, rolling hills across the valley from us set the perfect scene. It is one of the best, if not the best "cafe" we have visited. A dozen or so American ladies enter, chattering away like a flock of excited sparrows. Time for us to press on. Small stalls are also set up along the path, in the entrance to a drive of a house or the opening of a barn. All are lovely in their own way, with each trying to make a living on the Camino but the one we've just been in takes the biscuit.

We descend sharply now for quite a distance. The new, white town of Portomarin appears ahead of us across the valley. The old town lies submerged in the dammed reservoir below us.

*** *Debbie here again*: In the 1960s, the Mino river was dammed to create the Belesar reservoir, putting the old village of Portomarin underwater. The most historic buildings were removed brick by brick and reconstructed. When the reservoir is at a low level, the remains of the ancient buildings, waterfront and old bridge are still visible.

We cross a bridge over the reservoir…

…to be greeted by a flight of ancient steps up to an arch and the entrance to the town.

229

There is also the sound of bagpipes, flutes and drums coming from above the steps. Has the word of Dave and Steve's Camino gone before us? No, it's a music school practising. Our Albergue, Portosantiago is, yet again, up the hill and through the town. It's lovely. Ten bed dormitory, gardens with tables and parasols, a "chill out" outdoor lounge, with relaxing music playing and a foot massager. Dave pays the two euros, places his feet in and smiles. Bless him, he also did our laundry.

We've just had a lovely menu del dia for 9.50 euros. We have watched the pilgrims gather on the church steps like starlings getting the last of the sun's rays before they roost, and we are off to bed with a long day ahead.

Anyone Want a Hug?

Camino. Day 29. From Portomarin to Pontecampana. (32k).

Up and out at 06:45am, after another disturbed sleep. Why do so many people snore? I know that this subject has raised its head almost daily during my accounts but for those considering taking on this venture, you must, absolutely must take industrial earplugs with you. Anyway, 3, 2, 1, back on the Camino.

No chill in the air but still dark. We descend briefly towards the reservoir and turn right across a short bridge. Then the fun started. It was ten kilometres of constant climbing, some steep, some just a constant drag following the road but barely a car passed, it was so eerily quiet. Everywhere was covered in mist and then low cloud as we climbed. Our heads were wringing wet with sweat and moisture draped on every hair. The paths were poor and I for one was getting a little disillusioned. We ventured through a burnt pine forest and on to where the trees were green and the vegetation lush. Apparently, our research and Dave's map shows that this verdant area was "an outside brothel" in the 12th century. All quiet now, though. It amazes me how this particular fact was established, the mind boggles. Maybe it's now a 21st century "dogging area"? Sorry, it's been a long and lonely month. I'll try to concentrate.

On to Gonzar and our first stop. A bright, modern cafe on the left, with its lights lifting the mood of the gloomy, damp air. The warmth of the brew was extremely welcome and took a little of the chill from our bodies. On mornings like this, it's really difficult to decide whether to take your coat off and leave yourself shivering in a single, sodden top or to leave the coat on and continue shivering with all the moisture retained within. I kept mine on. As we were leaving the warmth and comfort of the café, a minibus pulled up and 12 American tourists alighted. All new kit and cameras at the ready. On the side of the bus was written "Cultural Walking Tours" by a company called Fresco.

Not much walking if you're in a bloody coach! I thought to myself.

We would see this bus park up later, a further 8k on at Arexe, where a picnic was being laid on for the "exhausted" American pilgrims. The constant chatter of American drawl coupled with the constant clatter of new walking sticks hitting the ground. All too much for us and we put our heads down, our arses up and powered past them into the silence of the distant trail. We arrived at their picnic site in Arexe way before the peace and quiet would be disturbed. We ate here too, not at the picnic site but just across the road as our energy levels were flagging. Egg and chips and eggs and bacon, both with a healthy half baguette. The day was getting hotter and the morning mist had long been burnt away, apart from deep below in the valleys. We walked through so many small hamlets with open barns, cows being milked, and a large boulder lay against a wall offering "Free Hugs" in several languages. We didn't get one.

Another noticeable thing today was the amount of eucalyptus trees in plantations which grew alongside the pine forests. Masses of them, tall and lanky, unlike Australian ones that spread their canopy. The foot paths were also littered with the bark shed by the eucalyptus trees. Not a koala bear in sight! Cunning blighters and so well camouflaged.

An ancient cross appeared on the left, which was all that was left of a pilgrim's hospital from hundreds of years ago.

Our next stop was at Palas de Rei. It's a large town and because of the heat, we stopped just before, near a sports complex. The kids across the road were playing football. Where do they get the energy in this heat? Black coffee and just enough time to catch my breath before the thought of putting my rucksack back on nearly reduced me to tears. I, for one, was completely exhausted and suggested to Dave that we strolled the remainder of the day. Just another six kilometres to go before we arrived at Pontecampana. What a difficult hour and a half it was. Both Dave and I were suffering now. Nothing in our legs, constantly taking on water and the sun beating down. In truth, I became bloody minded, almost crazy and just stomped my way through. This was a very long day. Then the clouds of despair parted. A small river ran through the lush, green fields, mature trees gave shade and two large brown cows munched lazily on the grass. The Albergue came upon us; it was called Casa Domingo. It was a picture. It's location was stunning and its inviting terraces and very old stone-built buildings just captivated you. The most picturesque Albergue on the whole Camino. Flower beds greeted us as we walked towards the bar/reception. Pilgrim passport stamped and a communal meal booked, we were escorted to our small dormitory. Perhaps only ten pilgrims would sleep here tonight. The historic stone walls and wooden roof all added to the atmosphere. I will come back here one day. I don't know when, but I will. It's simply that good and any potential pilgrim reading this should plan to stay here.

Our smalls were washed in the shower with us and hung out to dry in the baking sun (when I say "with us", I don't mean that Dave and I showered together!). Time for a lazy couple of hours. Marvin from Germany had also arrived and updated us on Lilly. Apparently, she has carried on walking, even with shin splints, and is going beyond Portomarin to Gonzar. What a crazy, stubborn young woman but in a pleasant way. Maybe we will see her in Santiago de Compostela. He also told us about an old stone house some 200 yards away down the field. This too was a pilgrim refuge but a little more exclusive and expensive. It only had a few rooms, more of a family hostel, really. Anyway, the house had apparently been an old mill house. The stream at the bottom of the field ran directly under the house. Part of the ground floor was now covered in glass through which you could see the old mill wheel workings and the stream flowing through.

We have seen dozens of what we thought were family shrines alongside virtually every house during recent days.

Dave and I have discussed the use of these "shrines", everything from chicken coops to family mini mausoleums for their ashes. None of which were correct. The answer will be in the next blog but no prize on offer.

On a slightly sour note, as some of our washing was returned to the dormitory, there was already a male pilgrim snoring his blinking head off just to the side of where Dave and I had our bunks. This was just a taster of what was to follow.

At 7:30pm, we had the communal meal. Maybe 20 of us. Two courses of soup, one cabbage, potatoes and lentils, the other pumpkin. How unusual. There wasn't an option, you got both. Salad, a vegetable dish and chicken, followed by a small portion of ice-cream and Santiago cake. Plus, wine and water. It was lovely.

Our bunks beckoned, still light, but sleep was really needed after this long day.

Only 62 kilometres to Santiago! And Dave planning every one of them.

Bank President to Pastor

Camino. Day 30. From Pontecampana to Ribadiso do Baixo. (23k).

Oh my goodness, what a night. Two beasts, the like of which we have never known, have competed for the World Snoring Championship. It was a dead heat. Awake from 11pm but up shortly after 5am, we rose and packed. It was 6am when we set foot on the road. Dave had his torch lit, strapped to his head and I followed in his footsteps. He was brilliant, "left here, right here, down the middle Steve". What a guy. A new game came upon us, or shall I say a different form of game, Night Rutting! 50 minutes of darkness. At this unearthly time, no bird song could be heard as we were walking even before they woke. The light changed as did our vision, the uneven ground and the stones rose to our eyes to make life easier. The birds awoke and our path was filled with a cacophony of chatter. I hate to be boring at this stage, but boy, we climbed again, what a blinking climb. It was like this for the rest of the day. Plenty of stops in this heat for the both of us. It's really hard work and although people say it gets easier, it doesn't.

More eucalyptus trees, still no koalas.

The pilgrims were congregating at the top of every climb. Consulting their maps. Left or right, they couldn't choose, but either direction ended up in the same place.

It was getting hot now and time to ditch the coats. The birdlife had come alive, robins, jays, crows, chaffinches and so many more. Dave and I kept walking, and walking. The draw of Santiago was like the beam of light from Mordor, relentlessly drawing us closer but at a seemingly quicker pace than the day before. No matter how far we went every cafe, bar or pilgrim rest point was closed. It was two hours and many false dawns before we found a cafe open in Melide.

Two coffees and two tea rojos later, with lovely cake served with each, we were off again. Today wasn't an unpleasant walk but four or five hills certainly

238

took its toll. On one of the final hills, a 10" lizard strolled down the road towards me as if he owned it. What a magnificent creature. Turquoise head with a vibrant green body and brown tail. Dave was behind with his phone/camera. I shouted but it was too late as the lizard disappeared into the hedgerow.

We approached Ribadiso do Baixo. All downhill to the river and the throng of buildings below. A set of steps invited pilgrims into the cool, refreshing waters. Oh, what a sight. However, not for us. We were another half a kilometre up the hill and across a main road to where our accommodation waited. No change there, then! Dripping with sweat, we fell into the reception. Booked in, escorted to a dorm of six beds and fingers crossed for a quiet night, we settled into a pleasant afternoon. From our lofty position, we could see the trail of pilgrims walking into the valley below and back up past us. The hills and surrounding countryside were magnificent.

We had a drink on the terrace and two ladies were at an adjoining table. We exchanged pleasantries and had a brief chat. They were called Katrina and Lesley, from the USA. Our T-shirts were on and Katrina asked us about their significance. We explained to her the charitable purpose of our Camino and she subsequently asked for the details of the orphanage. I had no idea what was to come at the end of the evening.

Late in the afternoon, Regina and Marvin joined us on the terrace. They too knew Kristina and Lesley and eventually we formed a group around a couple of tables.

We discussed many things, life, religion, the Camino and some personal things. As the conversation fragmented, I ended up speaking in depth with Katrina.

It transpires that she had joined CITI Bank in the USA some years ago. She had progressed to a stage where she was a president of one arm of the company. She had found her niche but had also found a fault in the cost saving aspect of the company, which conflicted with her view. She was more concerned with saving the jobs of others, who worked below her. A more moral and humane ideology. Basically, the hierarchy above her in the bank wanted to make people below her redundant in order to save money. Nothing new there but Katrina knew these people and how they needed work to support their families. She explained that she had to draw a line in the sand and had stood by her staff and convictions. She had also become aware of an urge deep inside her for something else. In brief, she was offered redundancy, accepted, and took three years out to train as a pastor.

She had also been one of 11 children and this is why she was attracted to Dave and me and our Camino journey. Several of her siblings were orphans, some Korean and others American, who were adopted by her parents.

In those few hours of sometimes intense conversation, I can honestly say that Katrina was one of the most instantly beguiling, intriguing and incredibly clever human beings I have ever met. You may call me shallow, but she really is impressive. Yes, the wine flowed, we all laughed at certain things, although her partner, Lesley, kept a reserved and demure distance. It was probably the most intellectually gratifying evening of the whole Camino. As I write this blog, both Lesley and Katrina are three feet away to my right. No snoring so far!

From left to right, Regina, Lesley, yours truly, Katrina, my Camino brother and Marvin.

Ah, before I forget…the answer to yesterday's blog question regarding the "mini crypt" in everyone's garden, the answer is that they are for drying corn in! Do you know that we have not seen one cornfield on the whole Camino! Nor will we.

You Really Shouldn't Drink on Duty!

Camino. Day 31. From Ribadiso de Baixo to Arca do Pino. (22k).

A lifeless, grey, morning greeted us as we left the Albergue at 06:50am. It's still not warm enough, at this stage, to walk without a coat at this time in the morning. Strangely enough, these short kilometre days are becoming really testing. We had climbed four hills before 08:30am. We were sweating like crazy. We had already cleared Arzua and were looking for a place to stop when Mr Noodles appeared from an Albergue door on the main road. We have seen him virtually every day on the Camino. He is from the far east, in his 50s and walks/rests on his own. He doesn't seem to talk to anyone but still greets us every time with a warm, sincere smile. I have christened him "Mr Noodles" as when we were in Castrojeriz on Day 13, he was there too. I was in the kitchen alongside him. He made a huge and I mean huge, portion of noodles in stock and heaven knows what else. There was enough for four hungry pilgrims. He sat, on his own, and devoured the lot.

Following his courteous, knowing smile, he waltzed off in his solitude.

We trotted on, that's a small lie, plodded on, following a brief stop. We climbed the fifth hill, at which point Dave quipped, 'Two more and we'll have something in common with Rome and Sheffield.'

The roaming paths were filling with pilgrims again, both long haul and short haul. Dave took a photo of a beautiful wisteria tree in full bloom. He then had to take a second, a few hundred yards on, where he could actually capture the full extent of its length and beauty.

I helped a group of Spanish pilgrims with their camera and took a photo of the three of them under the draped, lilac curtain. As we left one of the small roadside villages and turned into the final piece of forest, both Dave and I burst into laughter. On a stone table in a garden to our left sat three small dogs. None of them moved a muscle and to be honest, if Dave had not pointed them out, I would have thought they were garden ornaments and just drifted on by. Dave took a photo and no sooner had the shutter closed, they were off and across the lawn. As we passed them, they clearly heard another set of pilgrims approaching and we watched in amazement as they resumed their stone pose on the table.

The day was still grey and breathless, and we climbed, yet again, into a little unremarkable town called Arca do Pino. Off the main road and to our final Albergue on the Camino Frances, Albergue Edreida. It was a new building, functional and clean with hot, powerful showers. Two Spanish lads in their 20s entered with us. They had been close by for the last 10k; they were Antonio and Santi. Antonio was limping, suffering from a number of foot blisters. Out came the intense lavender oil for the 50th time on this Camino. It is remarkable stuff and an essential item for any would be pilgrim. He took it gratefully.

Showered, yesterday's blog completed, posted, we walked back to the main road and only source of "entertainment". We entered a pizzeria, ordered lunch and two beers. As we did so, we saw that an elderly member of the Guardia Civil had perched himself on a bar stool to our left. His sidearm nearest us and a healthy glass of red wine in front of him with a tapa. Who would think that the police could be on duty and drink? As if Dave and I ever did that. Well, not with a gun on our waist. He finished his "lunch" and ambled off to his vehicle parked in this sleepy town.

Within seconds, there was the whirring of a helicopter right above our bar. It was that close it sounded like it was landing on the roof. Seconds later, the siren of a fast approaching ambulance. The helicopter came into view meters away from our window which overlooked the valley. It was an air ambulance. We didn't go and find out what drama had unfolded. However, having finished lunch 20 minutes later, we walked down the street some 50 yards. The ambulance was just leaving the scene, our Guardia Civil man was being accosted by a female witness and concerned pilgrims finally wandered back along the street. I could almost read the officers mind, *You simply can't have a quiet drink on your own whilst working anymore.* Our best guess is that somebody, probably a pilgrim, had been knocked down.

It's time to shop for tea now as our Albergue has a kitchen. Pasta, what else, pasata, tin of mushrooms, two tins of fish, two tins of squid in ink, blue cheese, baguette, another cheeky white wine and cake from the Panadaria. 7.50 euros each. On the way back, and we weren't looking for this, honest, we found a funky little pilgrim bar only 50 meters at the back of our Albergue. It even had a path mown through the grass which took us along a short cut to our Albergue. It had been hidden from view earlier by a large fir tree, honestly. We just had time for a couple more beers. We were joined by Marvin, crazy Lilly and her new friend Laura, who is a young doctor from Dortmund. They have walked 36 kilometres today. Not bad with shin splints.

It then dawns on me that there's no hob in our Albergue! I leave my beer and go to check. No, there's no hob, but two microwaves. I've never cooked pasta in a microwave.

To my surprise, it worked. Perfectly cooked pasta, sauce of pasata with the fish, squid and mushrooms. Let me tell you my little Couch Pilgrims, I could do a cookery programme based on this. It would only be aired at 4am to put insomniacs to sleep, though! Dinner, however, was a little triumph.

Pilgrims around us are already talking about Santiago de Compostela and whether we like it or not, the tension and excitement is mounting. There's talk of a four-day festival (maybe that's why the flights have gone sky high, sorry about the pun), music in the streets, etc, etc. All Dave and I want is a steak and bed.

Oh, before I forget, we have been told that our friend, whom we have not seen for over a week, Ritchie from Germany, has had 50 euros stolen from his wallet a few days ago. His response was to say, 'Well maybe they needed it more than me!'

One final thing (footnote?), Dave's phone app, which tells us directions, kilometres, etc, also counts steps. To date, we have completed 1,081,766 steps on the Camino. We passed the million steps two days ago.

Sweet dreams.

Giving Dave My Best Sommelier Bollocks

Camino. Day 32. The Road into Santiago. (23k)

Well our dear friends, this is almost it.

Dave and I are up before six and out of the functional Albergue at 06:40am. Onto the main road leading out of this unremarkable town and into the fields and woods. Still dark and spooky. Weird noises all around. Blimey, pilgrims and more pilgrims at every corner. They converge, chatter, search for yellow arrows at every junction, and move on in a procession. The chilly and misty air means that Dave and I move on at a pace. Maybe it's also the pull of Santiago de Compostela. Once again, we are sodden. Inside our coats, sweat has ran down into our trousers, soaking wallets, tissues and watches. The watches we now carry in pockets as we have both managed to wrench the straps away from the faces as we repeatedly hauled our rucksacks off and on. Mine on Day One.

The hours and kilometres pass in somewhat of a blur today. Stop for tea and coffee as normal but we are swallowing up the ground. Lilly, Laura, Marvin and one or two other familiar faces appear en route but now we are lost in a sea of strangers.

The path leads off a roundabout and downhill for a few hundred yards. Bright orange lights, hundreds of them on huge barriers. A platform, level with the lights but set 40 feet up to our left on concrete posts. It's the end of the runway at Santiago airport.

Here's the ironic part. We are exactly level with the end and middle of the runway. The thunderous noise of jet engines fills the air and deafens us. This Goliath screams 100' above our heads out of the grey mist and down onto the tarmac. We can see the vapour trails left seconds behind. Wow, just fantastic. Almost! It's a bloody Ryanair flight. The Camino strikes again.

We press on up and down more hills, but we know now we have them beaten. Dave and I admit though that our legs are aching like heck; Dave's calves and my left thigh, the Camino is truly taking its toll. The final climb and to the top of Monte De Gonzo (Hill of Joy). The statue on the top looks like a big pair of owl's eyes as they peer through the dim light that surrounds Santiago de Compostela. We can now see its suburbs.

The city comes to us quickly. Lines of pilgrims, various rucksacks covered with rain protection. Every colour under the sun, every nationality you could think of. We follow the signs, or at least we thought we had, until an elderly lady shouts from her seat under a pergola in a park. Repeatedly, she tells us, 'It's the other road,' but in Spanish. A guy points to the brass shells embedded in the footpath, which shows that we should have crossed the road a hundred meters behind us. Gracias. We wave to the lady in thanks. Just a brief point, every city or major town has the brass shells embedded in its footpaths; it's not unique to Santiago.

Back on the route, it's becoming a pilgrim fest. Dave and I seem to be talking less and we can see the spires of the cathedral perhaps half a kilometre away. Time for some reflection and to control the emotions.

We arrive at the back of the cathedral and bump into Katrina, Lesley, Barbara and Jackie. The latter are two American ladies we first met over two weeks back. Hugs, congratulations and goodbyes all in the blink of an eye. Photos taken, we know we will not see Lesley and Katrina again. They have a connecting flight to Paris to catch this evening, before boarding a homeward bound flight to the good old US of A. Buen Camino, ladies.

Barbara informs us that there's a two-hour queue in the Compostela office. Dave and I descend into the cathedral square and have a manly hug. No tears, not quite, but I've found a "brother" for life.

One or two photos later, we make our way to the busy Compostela office. Not two hours, just 40 minutes, in a league of nations. I try to push Dave in front of me as we are next to go in. He won't have it and ushers me forward as the next counter become available. An Irish lady completes the documents. Plural, because both Dave and I want the certificates giving the distance travelled and another certificate stating where we started and finished along with the dates. We also buy tubes in order to protect them.

Out into the streets and on to find our hotel for the night, O Xardin de Julia. We arrive 20 minutes later. It's fine, nothing exotic, just fine.

Showered, refreshed but legs still aching, we're off and out for the 25-minute walk to the Apple shop. It's closed.

As I write this blog, we are sat in a cafe one minute away from the Apple shop and 20 minutes from the historic centre of Santiago, first pint in hand. I think we've deserved it.

Well, we've wandered around, been down to the Apple shop, who have kindly informed me that I need a new phone, just what I need! We've visited the cathedral and intend going back for the evening mass at 7:30pm. Time for a decent bottle of wine, my shout. We find a lovely bar in a narrow street not far from the cathedral. I treat Dave and myself to a beautiful bottle of Albariño, my favourite wine. Dave thoroughly enjoyed it and I gave him my best sommelier bollocks on what I knew about this Galician wine. Back to cathedral square, where we grab hold of a guy from Southampton called Rob. He does the gentlemanly thing and takes photos of us in our sponsored T-shirts in front of the cathedral.

We have been told to get in early for the mass, as it's usually packed. We arrive before seven but there's no great influx of pilgrims and worshippers.

At 7:30pm precisely, an elderly nun takes charge. Everyone to their feet, the service is in Spanish, but I can understand some of it as it's spoken slowly. Gilles, Sam and the drunken German lad from two weeks ago have joined us. All of a sudden, the nun leading proceedings starts to sing. The hairs on the back of my neck and Dave's, stood on end. She had the voice of an angel. I delved into my bag and took out the iPad, waited and pressed a video recording, just to capture her the next time she sang. I don't mind admitting I had tears rolling down my face. So, so much to be thankful for; 847 of them, to be precise. Sadly for us, the Botafumeiro was not lit or swung to and fro across the aisles. Maybe we will catch it midday Friday. The Botafumeiro is a vast metal incense burner. Once lit, it is hoisted above the congregation by several priests, who pull on the attached ropes as if they're campanology graduates. Their synchronised campanology subsequently sends the Botafumeiro careering into the void above the congregation below.

The service over and out into the daylight. Unfortunately, we have forgotten to explore the interior of the cathedral and do the traditional pilgrim "thing" of climbing the stairs behind the ornate statue of St James and touching his shoulders. Ah well, maybe next time, and there will be a "next time".

A quick beer with the three amigos followed, and Dave and I wished them all the best for the future, especially the tormented Gilles. We ventured into the market area, where we refrained from entering a pretentious bar. Instead, we found hidden cloisters, squares and alleyways in this historic city as we meandered amongst the hundreds of pilgrims and citizens who mingled there.

Down the hill we went to a bar we had seen earlier on the main road. It wasn't too far from our Albergue. Cooked octopus, a dish I'll never get tired of eating, a bottle of wine and we were ready to return to our hotel. What a lovely end to the Camino Frances.

I can't, at this moment, tell you what I've learned or what I will take forward in my life from this incredible experience. I just know that I will love Dave like a brother until my last breath. He is one of those special people you seldom get the chance to know in life.

Tomorrow will bring us to Finisterre and I've already said that I don't want it to be an anti-climax. Let's wait and see.

Return of the White Rhinoceros

Camino. The final 24 hours.

We had a bus to catch at 8am, which would take us to the bus station, so a quick hot drink and out into the sunshine. A short wait at the station and then we stepped onto a double decker super coach. Seats upstairs, Dave and I sat apart so that we could both have window seats for the best views en route to Finisterre. I have to say it was stunning once the mountains and forests had passed and we were given views of the coast. Lots of little fishing boats bobbed up and down in the coves, long, beautiful empty beaches with crashing, foaming waves. Green verdant hills rising gently behind the beaches with small villages dotted about. It was like being on the west coast of Scotland with Cornwall mixed in. The only thing was that you would have to multiply those images by ten. Galicia is simply beautiful. The journey took us two hours; it could have been two days, it didn't matter.

Rucksacks dropped off in our twin room in the Albergue, we found a small bar/cafe. I peered through the open door and saw that 50 feet away at the far end, was a wall of glass looking out at the Atlantic Ocean. That'll do nicely. Over a small beer and a bite to eat, Dave and I decided that we would set off for the lighthouse at the far end of Finisterre. Hundreds of years ago, when the world was believed to be flat, this was the last piece of the earth, until Mr C Columbus proved otherwise.

The hill rose gently for just over two kilometres. Trinket shops for the tourists and views that just made you gawp. Boiling masses of sea crashing into rocks which jutted out of the turquoise ocean. We simply could not take our eyes off it. A hundred meters away, a bar with a terrace. Where better to have a couple of small beers, put our feet up and collect our thoughts whilst staring at one of the most beautiful sights I can recall. There would be no traditional burning of clothes or running naked into the ocean. Both are illegal now and as it's a bank holiday weekend, the thought of four days in a Spanish cell soon curtailed any stupid urges.

This was the perfect end to our Camino. Could it yet surprise and astound us? Well, it wouldn't be our Camino if it didn't.

There she was, floppy hat, rucksack, orange vest top and scanning the horizon. It was Liz from South Africa. She saw us, let out a squeal and bounded up to the terrace. Hugs and kisses all round, none of us could get the right words out.

She told us that she was with her mum, Amelia and her partner, Hercules. They arrived, introductions made, and five more small beers ordered. Liz referred to us as her "Camino Dads", which was a really lovely thing to say.

They were having a champagne picnic and Dave and I had the headland to explore. We parted, but not before photos were taken and they were informed of where we would be eating around seven that evening, should they wish to join us.

The headland had a cement crucifix, which had been tarnished with some graffiti. A bronze pilgrim's boot, attached to a rock, took my eye and pilgrims everywhere were scrambling for the best vantage point from which to throw their final rock into the sea.

As we turned to leave, a green lizard maybe a foot or so in length decided to make an appearance on our path back up the rocks. He hadn't a care in the world and was more interested in flies and insects than us.

Back down to Finisterre and chance to take off our shoes and socks and paddle in the freezing Atlantic, which lapped into a sandy cove.

The restaurant that our hostess at the Albergue had recommended was on a large, terraced area in front of the port. Liz and family arrived as we were investigating, confirmed their desire to join us, so we booked a table for five that evening. As we enjoyed the warmth of the sun, and yes, another beer, we saw Santi and Antonio from a couple of days ago. Wouldn't you believe it, they had a hire car and offered to run us back to Santiago in the morning for free. We arranged to see them at 10:30am, a bit of a lie in, should we get carried away with the "Bon ami" around the dinner table later.

The evening arrived and we had a lovely meal with great company. It transpires that Hercules is a retired paediatric doctor who now has a consultancy role. However, his main passion in South Africa is to protect the white rhinoceros. He is the chairman of an organisation that does just that on a special reserve for orphaned rhinos. It has beautiful lodges and is north of Johannesburg (you can find it on *www.rooibewaria.co.za*, where there's also a photo of Mr Chairman himself). An open, sincere and generous offer was made by him to Dave and me in so much as we were welcome there any time for supporting Liz. It was a lovely evening in each others' company. A warm and genuine friendship developed. Hercules also paid for our meal on the understanding that we made a donation to our charities on his behalf. Consider it done, Hercules.

Friday morning came and sure enough our two young Spanish friends were there in a brand new, top of the range, Honda Civic. They greeted us and we gave them a decent bottle of red wine we had just bought as a "thank you". We knew they liked red wine as we had seen them drinking it the day before. It transpires that they are picking up three unknowns in Santiago who have booked a ride with them to Madrid via Blahblahblah.com. Apparently, any would be travellers go on this website to see if anyone can offer a lift to their destination. They then help with the cost. A modern version of hitchhiking, I suppose. The youth of today are so inventive.

The journey back to Santiago was quite quick, Rally Cross quick, and we soon found ourselves at the bus station. A firm shake of the hands and we were off in opposite directions. We had to find our bus to the airport, and they had others to collect.

The journey to the airport was on a cram packed coach in which we had to stand. Time seemed to drag as we held onto the bars above our head. Santiago airport is modern, clean and efficient. We found ourselves sat in the departure lounge with 11 hours to kill (no, we didn't get drunk!).

Dave visited the Duty Free shop and returned with a commemorative pin broach for me. I set about purchasing a new iPhone as the Apple Store in Santiago had said the one I'd started the Camino with had expired. I found an upgrade iPhone, a protective case and screen protector. I pressed the purchase button and sat staring at the further 400 euro figure I'd just spent. Oh well, somebody once told me, 'it's only money!'

I thought to myself, *I could just do with listening to some music. I know my phone doesn't work but I just wonder if it will play music?*

I unzipped my rucksack and rummaged around until I had it in my hand. Over to a table with a socket, I sat comfortably and switched on. Wouldn't you flaming know it, the whole bloody phone kicked into life. Photos, mobile signal – full coverage, the works! The only thing that didn't work was my blinking music. I simply couldn't believe it. It was clearly the condensation build up inside my coat that had soaked my phone, which, over the last two weeks or so, had dried out. I'm not sure whether Dave wanted to burst out laughing or crying as I'd moaned that much previously.

It was a short plane journey to Alicante, where we arrived at 1am. Janine and Debs picked us up. We both hobbled through the arrivals. It was a quiet car journey back, just like the one to Murcia at the start of this adventure. We were spent.

Closure

The time had arrived for the final bash, the official welcome home. Thursday, 24th May 2018. The street party, the gathering of the community, friends, neighbours, supporters, sponsors and family. The small road, or Campoverde Boulevard, as it's known, was closed off. The bars and restaurants filled the tarmac with tables, chairs and parasols. There was an air of excitement as the evening drew near.

I have to admit to being a little anxious and I think Dave was exactly the same. It was the culmination of everything, the planning, the work of the committee, the collection of funds from the incredibly generous people via website or collection buckets.

There was to be live music from Marie O'Hara and a band called Brodi, who had been booked by our resident landlord and landlady, Johnny and Louise. A raffle for the Real Madrid shirt, other football memorabilia and donated prizes, like a day trip on a boat for four people including constant cava, jet ski rides, massages, beauty treatments, free meals at local bars and a number of hampers stuffed with goodies. If I've forgotten any. I'm truly sorry but the generosity from everyone was overwhelming. I will come to the auction shortly.

To kick the evening off, there was Marie O'Hara. The booming, classical voice of an angel. For such a diminutive lady, she has an incredible voice. People were lapping it up. There must have been 200 guests all swaying and clapping to the melodies and singing along when they knew the words. Her first set lasted around 45 minutes and to complete it she performed "Nessun Dorma". I had been told just how good she was beforehand but nothing, absolutely nothing, prepared me for this. From the first note, everyone, to put it politely, gawped in shear amazement and silence beset the whole boulevard. The hairs on my neck stood on end and tears welled in my eyes and the eyes of many others. I swear to this day that I've hardly ever been so moved, recollection takes me to seeing Andre

Bocelli in Hyde Park, circa 1999, but this was special, it was on behalf of Dave and myself.

It came to a climax and was over. Everyone rose to their feet and she took the deserved applause.

I decided to take the microphone and thank her. The words, 'Well, how do you follow that?' had hardly left my lips when not twenty yards away a cat fight started between two women.

Pushing, shoving, some shoddy language and then a pint of beer thrown over one of the participants by the other. One or two men stepped in and order was quickly restored. Maybe some of the "singalong" was a little out of tune and one took exception.

I simply said, in reply to the previous question, 'That's not what I had in mind!'

Dave and I thanked Marie O'Hara for her first set and handed over to a group of locals who call themselves "Los Pistoleros". They are a group of maybe 20 people who perform the American trilogy. Authentic Western costumes and revolvers included. They entertained us all for half an hour before Marie O'Hara completed her second set. Once again, she had the audience captivated.

Throughout the evening, the raffle tickets were being sold like hot cakes. The Real Madrid shirt already had a bid of 1,000 euros and the atmosphere became fervent as our mate, and would be auctioneer, Kevin Leonard, took the microphone. He did a great job. The shirt had been shown around the audience, along with its authentication and Kevin opened the bid at the known 1,000 euros. There was a gasp amongst our little community gathered there in the gloom but we weren't done yet. If memory serves me right it raised 1,100 euros and went to a gentleman and his wife who had gone above and beyond in their support for our causes (the only reason I don't name them here is purely because they have a valuable item in their possession, much sought after in some areas of Spain and Campoverde is no exception).

People opened their wallets and their generosity poured out for the items on auction.

People were still coming up to Dave and myself during the evening and were stuffing donations in our hands as well. It was very humbling. The hammer came down on the last item. It had raised a good amount of cash, but we simply had no idea just how much.

Brodi, a really talented Irish band took up the reigns and continued to entertain the audience well into the evening, (past midnight and almost past bedtime). But before they did, Debbie Coupe announced the final total this night alone had raised, wait for it, drum roll, please… 3,260 euros. Blinking heck! Other expletives are normally available.

There is an acknowledgement page at the end of this book which details the committee, friends, relatives, supporters and sponsors but I must take this opportunity to thank each and every one of those not named. To those who baked cakes, carried tables and chairs, helped Dave and I prepare, sold tickets, gave words of encouragement, donated via website or bucket and any other way, WE THANK YOU! WE COULD NOT HAVE DONE IT WITHOUT YOU.

Now it's time for a well earned couple of pints and a round of drinks for the intimate group of people now gathered around Dave and myself.

Well, how else would you expect this journey for two pilgrims to end, other than having a pint in our hands.

Camino Footnote

I just want to take the time now, before the completion of my mind's meanderings, to explore some of the thoughts we had whilst on the Camino. In doing so, I do not want to find myself in hot water with the authorities but just highlight what came to us, and our fellow pilgrims, when we had time to settle down and open up with each other.

From my time in Spain, I have noticed that where money is concerned, the Spanish have methods of let's call it "creative accounting", along with the ability to turn a blind eye to the law where money or a "benefit" are concerned.

By example, I refer to the countless mayors of towns in Spain, government officials and the like, who, decade after decade, are in the news for taking "back handers" and conspiring with affluent people. This is hardly ever for the benefit of the majority. I also cite localised police chiefs who are found with their garage full of kilos of cannabis and hundreds of thousands of euros. All by way of bribes to turn yet "another blind eye" for the benefit of those who seemingly have more influence. In Spain, money is definitely king, irrespective of its source. Even when we purchased our first house here, we carried part payment, some 28,000 euros in cash held in a plastic shopping bag, into a meeting, where it was handed over as the "final payment". It or some of it also being referred to as "black money". You can make your own mind up.

I raise these points in wondering whether any of it applies to the Camino. Some of us, particularly those having the discussion in Sarria, muted this very point.

Dave and I were not necessarily "big spenders" on the Camino and for the benefit of this discussion, let's say that we were average spenders. Some pilgrims spend most nights in hotels and hostels, which are dearer than the Albergues and some don't enjoy a drink quite to the extent that Dave and I do. Then there are also around one third of pilgrims who only complete the 115 kilometres from

Sarria but are forced to get two stamps each day at cafes and bars (who made that rule and why?).

Dave and I spent 2,000 euros each, of our hard-earned money, in buying equipment, travel costs, accommodation, food and drink. During 2017, in excess of 300,000 pilgrims completed the Camino, let alone those who didn't. In simple mathematical terms, this amounts to around 600 million euros. It is forecast that even more pilgrims will travel the Camino this year.

We had to book into every Albergue with our English passport before our pilgrim passport would be stamped. I realise that there was a safety aspect to this, should there have been a fire, etc, but I also believe that there was a tax purpose to this as all of the Albergues, hostels' equipment stores and hotels were running businesses. I've just checked and the company tax rate is 25%. Following the intervention of the Spanish priest, Elijah Valina Sampedro, during the 1970s, in which he convinced the towns on the Camino to rejuvenate it, this would mean perhaps 50 years of the commercial Camino. Whichever way you look at it, there's an awful lot of money pouring into the coffers of Spain.

We earlier, on one of our days walking, alluded to the fact that the "Camino" meandered from village to village, where cafes, bars, trinket shops and Albergues all vied for your cash, and what's more, were successful. Some businesses were clearly decades old, whilst new enterprises sprang up alongside. There's clearly enough cash to go around! The question that shone like a lightbulb as we all discussed the matter was whether the Camino was a tourist trap? I'm not saying that James 1st was a fictional character, not at all, but did we actually walk HIS route or was there a more commercial reason behind our ventures?

My real bugbear in raising this issue is the fact that we saw so much of Spanish history just simply crumbling into the dust. Houses, so many of them, in the centre of towns, with roofs collapsed inwards. Their rotting beams at jaunty angles up against the crumbling interior walls. These walls, in turn, made of straw and mud, ruptured by decades of neglect and decay mounded up on the floors. Weeds, everywhere inside, exposed to the light that now cascaded daily through the void above.

Other houses, hundreds of years old, row after row of them, whole streets as in El Acebo, where terrace after wooden terrace, was held, limply, to the historic houses. How they didn't fall into the cobbled street below, God only knows.

It grieved me, angered me, to think that the "Camino Treasure Chest" was not being opened and reinvested in the repair of these magnificent buildings. Just how much does it cost to repaint thousands of yellow arrows which direct us? And, having hobbled down every path, I can say that there isn't much maintenance required here either.

If there is a restoration programme, I personally didn't see any evidence of it. What a crying shame. Surely these deserted buildings would be a "tourist trap" for any would be pilgrim if restored to their magnificent, original state. Hours could be spent seeing the real, historic Spain whilst walking the route, and paying for the privilege. A constant pilgrim's museum. Who knows, it may be another cash cow?

Were we being cynical in Sarria? Yes!

Could we care less? No!

Would we change anything? No, not about the Camino experience.

Would we do it all again? Absolutely and without hesitation!

Apologies! I love the Camino in all of its facets. It's probably the best adventure of my life and to this day, it still courses through my veins. In fact, as I bring this book towards its close its 12 months since that last day and I've had the inside of my right arm tattooed with the crucifix of St James and a string of scallop shells. I would recommend it (not a tattoo) to anyone.

Just to make you all smile, well maybe. Since completing the Camino, both Dave and I have been in email contact with just a couple of our fellow pilgrims, Lilly and Liz. It transpires that everyone, yes everyone, we met thought that Dave and I were gay pilgrims. The irony of that is, whilst we aren't (not that there's anything wrong with being gay), both Dave and I thought that poor Gilles and his broken marriage may have been because of the fact that he had not acknowledged, or indeed, had chosen to ignore, what we perceived to be his blatant bisexuality.

The Camino De Frances in Figures

2,000 euros each.

San Juan Pied du Port to Santiago 32 days.

847 kilometres walked (via Dave's GPS).

26.5 kilometres per day on average.

Eight days of rain.

Two days when it snowed.

9.5 kilos on our backs.

Two blisters.

At least four peaks climbed all around the height of Ben Nevis.

Weight loss – 10 kilos.

1,270,500 steps (give or take, not including socially at the end of the days).

Times I replied bloody "Buen Camino"; hundreds.

Bugs squished underfoot, none, not a one, even accidentally.

Incredible people met…dozens.

Memories…more than the number of steps!

New "brother" and friend for life: 1.

Charitable funds raised, 10,000 euros, split between AECC Cancer and San Jose de Obrero Orphanage.

Regrets: 0.Times I nearly gave up: 1.

Dave and I have spent hours scanning the hills and scenery in front of us. We saw paths, many paths. Some straight ahead, uphill and daunting, another to the right, flat and uninteresting, one to the left, slightly hidden by trees and full of mystery. With the best will in the world, we never seem to pick the one we are on until we turn at a hedgerow which shows a different path altogether.

I have asked myself, 'IS THIS LIFE?' Do we ever know which path lies ahead, which is best? Which indeed to choose. All I can say is that you will find yourself on the right path when the time comes. But you had better be prepared for the daunting, the mundane, the mysterious or the exciting. Whichever it is, it is YOUR path. No matter what it holds, good, bad or indifferent. Just make sure you choose the right one and enjoy it.

There's an innocence on the Camino. The shackles of modern society are broken. You are set free. The days on the Camino come and go, merge into one, but some of the people you meet and the memories you share will stay with you forever.

People say, 'Make the most out of life.' Post-Camino, I now believe that "life makes the most out of you".

My next adventure? Who knows? Maybe I'll find myself north of Johannesburg, looking after baby white rhinos!

Buen Camino.